P9-BYT-135

Educating for the 21st Century

Educating for the 21st Century

The Challenge for Parents and Teachers

Mark H. Mullin

Madison Books
Lanham • New York • London

Published by Madison Books
4720 Boston Way
Lanham, Maryland 20706

3 Henrietta Street
London WC2E 8LU England

Distributed by National Book Network

The paper used in this publication meets the minimum requirements of American National Standard for Information Sciences—Permanence of Paper for Printed Library Materials, ANSI Z39.48–1984. ♾™
Manufactured in the United States of America.

Library of Congress Cataloging-in-Publication Data

Mullin, Mark H., 1940-
Educating for the 21st century : the challenge for parents and teachers / Mark H. Mullin.
p. cm.
Includes bibliographical references (p.) and index.
1. Education, Secondary—United States—Aims and objectives. 2. High school students—United States—Conduct of life. I. Title.
II. Title: Educating for the twenty-first century.
LA222.M84 1991 373'.011'0973—dc20 91-635 CIP

ISBN 0–8191–8062–9 (alk. paper)

British Cataloging in Publication Information Available

For Martha Jane

Contents

Foreword

The pages that follow contain the thoughts, hopes, and concerns of someone who has spent more than twenty years in secondary education preparing youngsters for college and university. Because I have been a headmaster for more than a decade, I have of necessity been in contact with every aspect of school life. On the other hand, it has been many years since I have had an opportunity to study education in a formal and systematic way. Therefore, what you will read are reflections, not research. These words come from the heart and mind of someone trying to understand how best to serve students during the last decade of this century.

There are two most important roles for a headmaster. The first is to have in his own mind, and to share with others, a vision of what the school and all the individuals in it might become if they reach for the very best. The second is to say "thank you" on behalf of the school. Of course, there should be a "thank you" to all those who support the school financially. Their help is essential. Even more important is gratitude to the men and women of the faculty and staff who receive such small financial rewards, but who do so much to help young people grow and develop. All who work at the school are thankful to those wonderful volunteers—parents, alumni, friends who give so much of their time and talent to the school. Heartfelt are appreciation and congratulations to students when they perform with distinction. And if the headmaster is a believer, he will frequently thank God. On some days the gratitude will be that he is being allowed to spend his life in such a challenging and rewarding profession. On other days the thanks will be that the incredibly volatile mixture of competing egos, goals, and demands for time that comprise a school community has not exploded into chaos.

Because the rest of these pages will deal with my thoughts and vision of education, it seems appropriate that in this Foreword, I express my gratitude. I give a most heartfelt thank you to the Governing Board of St. Albans School, which graciously granted me a sabbatical during the spring of 1988. During that period when I was freed from the day-to-day operations of the school, I had time for reflection and writing. I am particularly indebted to E. Tillman Stirling, Chairman of the Governing Board, John F. McCune, Head of the Upper School, A. Wayne Gordon, Head of the Lower School, and Maurice K. Heartfield, Administrator, for the extra burdens they assumed during my absence. I have great gratitude to the faculty and staff of St. Albans School, with whom I share the great adventure of educating young people. Special thanks are certainly due to Wayne C. Thompson of the Virginia Military Institute, who first encouraged me to do this writing and then provided very thoughtful criticism of the manuscript. Paul G. Leonhard, Philip Smith, Lynn Gemmell, and James E. Lyons made many valuable suggestions. Of particular help was Kathy Diehr of St. Albans School, who was invaluable in the editing of this work. My deep personal thanks go to all my teachers who gave so much of themselves to me. Alma and Joe Mullin were the most important teachers in my life. Finally, my gratitude to Martha Jane who has shared with me the joys and cares of helping young people grow up in a unsteady and confusing world.

Chapter One

Children of the Moon

In the summer of 1969 I lifted my two-month-old daughter out of her crib and held her on my lap in front of the television set. Of course I knew that the flickering image had no meaning for her, but I wanted it to be possible for her to say, years later, "I watched the first time a human being walked on the moon."

In due course, that daughter grew up and toward the end of the '80s graduated from high school. Most of her college career took place during the '80s, even though her graduation will occur in this decade. She and her contemporaries are the last of the "earthlings." The children born after them are the first human beings whose entire lives will be spent after the conquering of the moon. They, indeed, are children of the moon.

I believe that the year 1969 is an historical milestone, such as 1066 or 1492. Those born after 1969 will have their undergraduate experience during the last decade of the century. We who care for them, whether as parents or teachers, must ask: "What will these young people, children of the moon, need in secondary school to prepare them to be college students in the 1990s?" The even more important question is: "How can we best prepare them for adulthood in the twenty-first century?" It will be then that they will come into positions of responsibility. These are essential questions for the welfare of our children and the welfare of our society.

During the past few years a number of books on education have caught the attention of the American public. Some have dealt with the organization of American public education; *A Nation at Risk*[1] and *The Shopping Mall High School*[2] have been the most widely received. Even more striking has been the best-selling status achieved by two books on the content of education. E. D. Hirsch in *Cultural Literacy*[3] makes a strong case for a common body of knowledge that is shared by all educated members of a society. Hirsch argues that shared knowledge is essential for communication among persons in a society because all communication presumes that a number of terms and ideas have meaning to both parties. Without this shared knowledge, every reference or illustration would have to be fully explained. Because we do not explain every reference we use in normal conversation, lack of cultural literacy can result in partial incomprehension or confusion. Hirsch believes that unless a grounding in a certain amount of cultural literacy is achieved by the fourth grade, it will be very difficult for someone to acquire the needed information later. Certainly, according to Hirsch, high school is too late.

At the other end of the educational process, Allan Bloom in *The Closing of the American Mind*[4] criticizes the colleges for their failure to give students the philosophical and historical background necessary to make informed choices about the nature of the good life. In fact, according to Bloom, most higher education has not even shown students that the good life is something about which one can make rational inquiry and then thoughtful decisions.

By the questions they have raised and the discussion they have provoked, both Hirsch and Bloom have given important stimuli to American education. But they have not given us careful analysis of secondary education. In the pages that follow, I will address some of the questions of secondary education. It is true that the most important learning takes place at the younger ages. And it is equally true that deep intellectual work is unlikely to occur before a student is engaged in higher education. Yet the secondary years are vital. They are a period of great change for a young person. In American society students enter high school as children; yet, before or just after they leave, they are given adult freedoms, even if they are not given responsibilities.

Certainly, the most important challenge facing American education is how to create programs in public schools which will prepare some students for higher education while preparing others to become productive citizens with no further formal education. The difficulties of this task are immense. There are questions of motivation, allocation of resources, vocational preparation, and most important, a vision of the American dream of equality of opportunity. America's ability to meet the educational needs of all our young people may be the single most determinant factor for our relative standing in the world.

The need to provide useful education for those who will not go on to college, and the organization of our public schools to meet this challenge, are issues outside the scope of this essay. I will describe secondary education for college-bound students. It is imperative that we send students to college who are as well prepared as possible. Because this is now such a large number of our young people, it is essential that our society continually evaluate how best we should prepare our children for higher education.

Although I graduated from a public high school, all my professional life, including more than a decade as a headmaster, has been spent in independent schools. While it is true that independent schools have special advantages (and special problems), I believe that my observations will be true for most college-bound secondary school students. I am not writing about schools, but about those who are preparing for college in many different sorts of schools. The subject of this inquiry is the education that they must have to be prepared for college and to be responsible adults in the twenty-first century.

Because of their birth after the moon landing, I have called those who will be in college during the 1990s children of the moon, and it is their secondary education I will consider. Regardless of whether these young people are really different from the earthlings who came before them, the voyages into space may illuminate the special challenges facing educators and parents during the 1990s. Three aspects of space exploration are most significant: knowledge, the oneness of our earth, and the fragility of the planet.

Knowledge

The first and most obvious lesson of the moon trips is that knowledge, particularly scientific knowledge, is expanding at a truly astronomical rate. Space travel would be impossible without the vast increase in technical knowledge acquired since World War II in such fields as computers, physics, metallurgy, rocketry, medicine, radio and television communication, and astronomy. It is a truism that such knowledge feeds on itself. Every space trip that new knowledge makes possible produces even more information. The space flights symbolize and help us to understand the fact that the sum total of human knowledge doubles in less than two years. What a different world it was for teachers when the basic knowledge shared by all educated people was a relatively fixed body of material. The task then was simply to convey that knowledge to one's students. But now new information is being discovered so fast that it is probable that a student (as well as his teacher) will know a smaller percentage of all human knowledge when he graduates than when he entered secondary school. In this Alice-Through-the-Looking-Glass world, the task for the educator becomes one of being very selective about what information to present to the student while frantically trying himself to keep up with the new information. Moreover, it is clear that the knowledge explosion means that secondary education must not only prepare students for college, but must also prepare them to continue learning throughout their lives. To look at the most obvious example, when I graduated from college, I knew no one among my 1,200 classmates who had ever used a computer, and word processors did not even exist. By the time of our twenty-fifth reunion, many of our classmates regularly used a computer and an even larger number could not imagine life without a word processor.

The need for lifelong learning is accompanied by a need to be constantly adjusting to change. To reach the age of eighty is something of an accomplishment, but by no means it is an unusual one. Think of a student who entered secondary school at the time that mankind first achieved the dream of the millennia, to defy gravity and to fly. That same person would not have turned forty when Charles Lindbergh showed that the Atlantic was not a significant barrier to travel. The secondary student of 1903 would have been eighty when men really broke the bonds of earth and walked on the moon. What incredible change he had to adjust to between the time he entered high school and when he reached old age! Change in mankind's ability to fly both symbolizes and caused tremendous changes in society. If change was rapid for those who were in high school just after the turn of the century, the rate of change will be, as it were, at the speed of light for those who are in high school in the 1990s. Thus education must prepare them not only for an ongoing explosion of knowledge, but for the changes in society and culture that the new knowledge will produce.

One Earth

The second lesson of space exploration is a visual one. It is from space that the oneness of the earth is most clear. Michael Collins, who was orbiting the moon while Neil Armstrong took man's first step on the moon, has written movingly of the impact the sight of the earth from the moon had on him:

"I can now lift my mind out into space and look back at a midget earth. I can see it hanging there, surrounded by blackness, turning slowly in the relentless sunlight. I think the view from 100,000 miles could be invaluable in getting people together to work out joint solutions, by causing them to realize that the planet we share unites us in a way far more basic and far more important than differences in skin color or religion or economic system. That all-important border would be invisible, that noisy argument suddenly silenced. The tiny globe would continue to turn, serenely ignoring its subdivisions, presenting a unified facade that would cry for unified understanding, for homogeneous treatment. The earth *must* become as it appears: blue and white, not capitalist or Communist; blue and white, not rich or poor; blue and white, not envious or envied. Of course, we could always pass out Whole Earth photographs and have everyone study them, and if there is any truth in my 100,000-mile premise, the results should be the same. Unfortunately, it doesn't work that way. Seeing the earth on an 8×10-inch piece of paper, or ringed by the plastic border of a television screen, is not only not the same as the real view but even worse—it is a pseudo-sight that denies the reality of the matter. To actually be 100,000 miles out, to look out four windows, and find nothing but black infinity, to finally locate the blue and white golf ball in the window, to know how fortunate we are to be able to return to it—all these things are required, in addition to merely gauging size and color. While the proliferation of photos constantly reminds us of the earth's dimensions, the photos deceive us as well, for they transfer the emphasis from the *one* earth to the multiplicity of reproduced images. There is but one earth, tiny and fragile, and one must get 100,000 miles away from it to appreciate fully one's good fortune in living on it."[5]

The space program has not only given us a visual image of the oneness of the earth, it has helped us to create that oneness. Satellite transmission, which is sometimes placed on and even repaired by the space shuttles, has made instantaneous communication possible throughout the world. An event can be seen and heard anywhere in the world the same moment that it is occurring, and information can be shared equally rapidly. A hundred or so people watched Columbus land in the new world; half a billion people watched Neil Armstrong walk on the moon. Nor is the oneness of the world limited to information or visual images. The technology of modern travel, the economic interdependence of the modern world, and the threat of annihilation, using space age weapons, all help to emphasize the oneness of the earth.

This oneness, however, creates special problems for

educators. In the past their task was to introduce young people into the national culture. Students were to be taught the history, literature, and traditions of one culture. Hirsch argues that such knowledge makes up cultural literacy. For the children of the moon, that is no longer adequate. During their adulthood, they will be dependent upon and constantly interacting with people of other cultures. Therefore, they must have an understanding and appreciation of many cultures. Educators must now make difficult decisions about the application of that most precious resource—time. They must decide how much of a student's time should be spent developing the necessary grounding in his or her own culture, and how much should be spent exposed to other cultures.

This Fragile Earth

The third lesson of the moon is a subtler one, yet it is the most important one. Michael Collins also wrote:

"If I could use only one word to describe the earth as seen from the moon, I would ignore both its size and color and search for a more elemental quality, that of fragility. The earth appears 'fragile' above all else. I don't know why, but it does. As we walk its surface, it seems solid and substantial enough, almost infinite as it extends flatly in all directions. But from space there is no hint of ruggedness to it; smooth as a billiard ball, it seems delicately poised in its circular journey around the sun, and above all it seems fragile."[6]

The fragility of the earth should make us all wrestle with the ethical questions in two important areas. Clearly, the ecological system that supports life on earth is fragile and is now endangered. We must make difficult choices between our desire to use the resources of the earth for mankind's benefits and the danger that in doing so, we will destroy them or even ourselves. Certainly technological information will be necessary to make these choices, but so will goodwill and a willingness to set the common good above self-interest. Thus, moral reasoning and the application of moral principles must be an important part of the decision-making process. If the fragility of the earth raises long-term ecological questions, instantaneous destruction by nuclear war raises even more urgent questions. Once again, the right decisions require both technical information and moral concern. Do our schools prepare students to make moral decisions?

I would argue that for those who will be in secondary school and college in the 1990s, the preservation of the ecological system and the avoidance of nuclear destruction may be the most important ethical issues. While the reduction of tensions between the United States and the Soviet Union has eased the nuclear threat, the early 1990s showed the potential that many countries have to disturb world peace and indicated how dangerous nuclear proliferation would be.

To say that there is little consensus in our society for standards of right and wrong, of acceptable and unacceptable behavior, would be a great understatement. There is even less consensus about how such standards are derived, who should set them, and how they should be enforced. However, these unresolved dilemmas merely emphasize that for the children of the moon, moral thinking and acting are of the utmost importance simply because of the interdependence of all people.

The most obvious example of interdependence is that moral decisions about sexual behavior, combined with jet age travel, have created the worldwide problem of AIDS. Our students face greater moral uncertainty in both public and private morality than any other generation before them. Certainly parents are deeply worried about the moral development of their children. A number of polls have shown that the lack of effective moral education is the greatest concern parents have about the education their children receive. The fragility of the earth, seen most dramatically from the moon, is a reality, and it is also a symbol of our own fragility. Both the preservation of the earth and the development of a meaningful individual life demand ethical thinking and ethical action.

In October 1990 I jointed eight public school principals on a study mission to the Soviet Union as guests of the State Committee for Education. In a meeting with Dr. Nickolai Nechajev, Director of the Main Department of General Secondary Education, I was fascinated to hear him say that the Soviet Union will be putting considerably more emphasis on moral education. He spoke of the need for moving away from the training of servants of the state to the development of humanistic individuals. It appears that even in very different societies, those who think about the world our present students will inherit see the need for them to develop moral strength.

Looking Forward

In the pages that follow, I will look at several aspects of secondary education. I will consider the adolescent world in the 1990s, what cultural forces shape the lives of our students, and what special problems they face. Since parents are the single most important influence in the lives of children, I will give some thought to parenting in the 1990s. Moreover, parents will demand an increasing role in the education of their children. This fact will need careful consideration, for it will significantly influence secondary education. Then I must hazard some observations about the world our students will inhabit when they become responsible adults in the twenty-first century. This must obviously remain the most tentative and speculative of chapters. Trying to foresee future conditions is always a dangerous game, but to fail to attempt it is even riskier. We must give thought to what we are preparing our students for, and perhaps a little stargazing is not out of place as we think about the education of the children of the moon. The next step, of course, will be to analyze what secondary school curriculum will best meet the needs of the students of the 1990s and prepare them for both college and the twenty-first century. This will involve us in the debate already joined by Hirsch, Bloom, and others. It is important that we wrestle with the very difficult issue of how schools can engage in moral education. Here the answers may not be clear, but the problems and possibilities need to be elaborated. Above all, it must be argued that the search for answers is not only a worthy endeavor but an essential one if we are to serve our students well. The Socratics called this "philosophy," but we must see it as essential knowledge for the children of the moon. We cannot merely leave these questions to the philosophers as we go about our busy lives. Finally, I would like to draw some observations based on my personal experiences as headmaster of St. Albans School in Washington and set before us what I think are the most important challenges in secondary education in the 1990s.

The conquest of the moon happened just before the secondary and college students of the 1990s were born. This milestone in the history of mankind symbolizes three important problems for educators. How can we help students cope with an ever-increasing amount of knowledge and the societal changes that new knowledge brings? How can we prepare students to live in an ever-shrinking world and understand a variety of cultures? How can we prepare students to be moral men and women who can preserve the earth and live worthwhile lives on "this fragile earth, our island home?"[7]

Chapter Two

Those Who Learn

I joined the faculty of a New England boarding school in 1968. At that time I had spent a number of years in graduate school. Among the other new teachers was a young man who had graduated from college the previous June. He told me that during his freshman year in college he knew no one who had even tried drugs. During his senior year he knew no one who had not used drugs. This story reminds us how quickly the attitudes and behavior of students can shift. As I describe the students of the 1990s, I am actually writing of those who were in secondary school in the late 1980s, for those are the ones I know. If there should be a rapid shift in student life, my words will soon be out of date, but it is also true that swings in the nature of students such as the one that occurred in the late 1960s are very rare. Therefore, it is likely that many of the student characteristics of the late 1980s will continue to be seen in those who follow them during the 1990s.

For several years I had the enjoyable privilege of sitting on the Mid-Atlantic Marshall Scholarship Selection Committee. The scholarship provides all expenses for two years of study at a British university for American students who have graduated from college. As we read the more than one hundred essays by candidates and interviewed about twenty of them each year, we were constantly struck with the very high level of performance and sophistication of these college seniors. Two of us on the committee held Marshall scholarships in the early 1960s. We often laughed when we thought of the rather pathetic essays we had submitted and how naive we must have sounded during our interviews. We realized that if we had been competing against today's top college students, we would not have had a chance. This experience with college seniors points to a fact that is also true for today's secondary students. The good ones are very good—they work hard, they take more advanced courses than their predecessors did, they have an intellectual sophistication and a breadth of knowledge that many of us who are now adults did not acquire until we were well along in our college careers. Moreover, they often combine academic excellence with significant accomplishments in some other area of school life, whether it is athletic, artistic, musical, or journalistic.

One encouraging trend is that today's students cannot be stereotyped by their nonacademic interests. I have a friend who claims that his college admission in the 1950s was due to a chance remark. The admissions director of an Ivy League college was in the office of the college guidance counselor of my friend's school. The admissions director commented favorably on an oil painting hanging on the wall.

"Oh," replied the college counselor, "that was painted by our all-league tackle on the football team."

"I'd like to meet him," said the admissions director. "We don't get many tackles who can paint."

Indeed, the admissions director did meet and later admitted my friend. That story could not be told in the early 1990s because football players who paint are not an unknown breed. Yet I fear that soon they may become so again. If this happens, it will not be because of the kind of stereotyping of the 1950s into "jocks" and "artsy." It will be because of increased pressure for college admission. Secondary students are hearing from more and more college admissions officers that highly selective colleges are looking for students with real commitment and expertise in one area, rather than involvement in many areas. Says one college admissions officer: "The colleges are not looking for well-rounded students. They are looking for well-rounded bodies made up of individuals with special interests and accomplishments."

I believe that the best of today's students are tremendously talented and often quite sophisticated. It is perhaps more difficult to assess how the average college-bound youngster compares with his or her predecessor. But for all secondary students, there are some important characteristics that educators and parents must recognize, and I will focus on three of them. One has been produced by technology, another by the change in the family, and the third by the way young people relate to each other.

Visual Media

Foremost among the descriptions of this generation of students is the fact that they are audiovisual creatures. I was fourteen when my family acquired its first black and white television set. An exciting Saturday night was George Gobel followed by *Your Hit Parade*. There will be high school students in the 1990s who say: "I was fourteen when my family acquired its first compact disc player." But these are young people for whom television, along with other high-tech means of communication, has always been a part of their lives. Allan Bloom[1] has a fascinating chapter on the effect of popular music on teenagers. I commend that chapter to all educators and parents. Yet television is the most pervasive and powerful media influence on our children.

Much has been written about the effects on children of watching violence on television, but I do not believe that that is its major impact. Instead, I would point out four general ways that television influences all young people. The first I would call passivity. It has been estimated that by the time the average American is fifteen years old, he or she has watched 15,000 hours of television. While this is probably too high a figure for college-bound teenagers, even they will have watched many thousands of hours. For those who are intending to go to college, most of those hours will not come from homework time, although there are many critics who believe that American schools do not give enough homework. Instead, most of this television time will have replaced play and family time. It is when there is free time that it is easier to flip on the television or put in a movie cassette than it is either to be creative enough to invent a way to play alone or to find friends with whom to play.

Spending significant amounts of time watching instead of playing has important consequences. It is a passive, spectator activity, and any involvement is vicarious. The viewer learns to receive pleasure without personal involvement. In effect, a television watcher says: "Entertain me, with no effort on my part, or I'll change channels (or videocassettes)." When this attitude—that all must flow to my liking, to my pleasure—is repeated for thousands of hours during childhood and adolescence, it must indeed teach a subtle but powerful lesson. Stated in its baldest form (and few people ever state it this way) the lesson is: "I have a right to be entertained, to be pleased, with very little effort on my part. And if my environment does not please me, it is a simple matter to change the environment (i.e., channel or cassette)." By the time they reach high school, the children of the moon have had thousands and thousands of hours of conditioning to such thinking. Those of us who are teachers certainly see the effect of it in students whose attitude is that they do not have a responsibility to learn, but the teacher has a responsibility both to teach and to entertain. Fortunately, many students are able to overcome this conditioning and they do accept responsibility for their education, but it takes maturity and a sense of purpose to do so.

While this attitude has important implications for those of us who teach today's students, I think it has even greater effects on their personal relationships. The language of television viewing is adapted to persons—"She really turns me on" or "When my old man starts in on my grades, I just tune him out." Even more significant than language is attitude. If a program does not please, switch channels (or cassettes). If a relationship does not please, switch relationships.

Another form of conditioning produced by the visual media is that commercial television stops the program every twelve minutes for a series of commercial messages. Thus Americans are conditioned from early childhood to have twelve-minute attention spans, followed by a dash to the kitchen. Those of us who preach to modern Americans adjust to this by timing our sermons to be twelve minutes long. The problem is more difficult for the classroom teacher who must fill a period of forty-five or sixty minutes. The wise teacher changes the routine or the lesson or the mode of presentation every twelve minutes. It is too soon to know, but if a generation grows up spending more time with videocassettes and cable television, which present uninterrupted action for two hours, there may be a new set of conditions. However, even the movies seen on cassettes change the setting frequently to maintain viewer interest. It has been my observation that movies made for television rather than for first distribution in theaters change the settings even more frequently. But the most frequent changes of setting, about one every two minutes, are on the television "soaps" which jump from location to location and character to character with a rapidity that ensures that only the devoted followers (that is the idea, after all) can understand who is doing what to whom.

The fact that television produces a need for change results in effects other than short attention spans. It has helped develop a generation for whom the new, the novel, is always to be sought, to be expected. Just before today's secondary students were being born, I was supervising a dormitory at a boys boarding school. After the second lunar landing, the moon walk was scheduled to be broadcast very late at night. I told the boys in my dormitory that they had my permission to stay up late and watch it. They replied: "Oh, we don't want to stay up and watch. We saw the first moon walk." If pictures of human beings walking on the moon are not exciting enough to stay up for, what is?

Finally, while we are considering the passivity produced by television, we must return to the fact that so much television viewing occurs during what could be play time. It is during play time rather than study time that children most learn how to interact with each other, how to share, how to take turns in being dominant, how to cooperate. Yet if much of that time is spent passively watching, even in the company of others, lessons on the essential skills of give-and-take may be lost. This is clearly most important in young children, but I find it a sad picture to see a group of teenage boys and girls all staring at a screen and not interacting.

A few of today's youngsters allow computers to replace

personal relationships in the same way that television may. While operating a computer is considerably less passive than watching television, it can still keep a young person from developing friendships and interactions necessary for normal personal growth. A computer reacts the way *you* program it. Other people act in less predictable ways. The danger of isolation is even greater for those who are involved with computers because parents often encourage home computer use. They believe that it will be useful for school and even provide employment, as it often does.

I know of a very bright (and very rich) high school student who never went to the home of another teenager or had a friend to his house. He spent all his time with his computer. He made a number of friends with whom his computer "interfaced" and with whom he was in frequent contact. Ironically, he had never seen these "friends" or even heard their voices. This is obviously an extreme case, and I do not want mean to imply that students should not learn to use, or even enjoy, computers. But it is important to recognize that both television and computers can keep young people from experiencing the give-and-take of normal human relationships and this may have significant consequences in later life.

If a self-gratifying passivity may be one effect of television, a stilted way of viewing the world may be another. I indicated earlier that many of us are impressed with the sophistication of today's best students. In some respects television may be partly responsible for their precocious achievement. From early ages, children are exposed to all the world with its multiplicity of cultures, its controversies, and its goodness and evil. They are inevitably less insular, less certain that one group has a monopoly on truth than those who came before them. The fact that they grew up exposed to so many interpretations of what is right and wrong will have implications which we must consider in a later chapter. But for now we must look at another effect.

The brightest and best read of our students use the exposure of television as a base for developing a thoughtful and sophisticated view of the world. I fear that this is not true of all our students. While providing broad exposure, television encourages very superficial and shallow analysis of problems, whether public or personal. On the evening news only two minutes (or at most five) can be allotted to highly complex national or international situations. During an election, it is the funny quip or barbed attack of a candidate that is aired, not his carefully reasoned and thoughtful analysis of issues. Youngsters are led to believe that difficult problems have simple answers. It is not surprising that during the years those who will be secondary school students in the 1990s were first watching television, the President of the United States was a former television actor.

Perhaps the effect of the portrayal of conflict on television is most instructive. The camera instinctively turns to action, and violence provides the most action. If 200,000 people gather for a peaceful demonstration, the fight between four people (0.002 percent) that leaves one bloodied and one injured will probably be given more air time than a serious speech that thoughtfully deals with the issues. The impression given to even the most discerning viewer must inevitably be somewhat distorted.

While critics of television are concerned with violence or crime shows, the violence on the news is equally influential. The reality of violence watched during our first televised war certainly affected the way Americans thought about the Vietnam conflict. But in the intervening twenty years another phenomenon has occurred. We have seen so much violence on the news that we are hardly shocked by it. During the mid-1970s my family was watching a special on Winston Churchill. It began with a scene of his casket being brought ceremoniously by boat along the Thames. My young son, who had seen films of two Kennedy and one King funerals, asked me, "Did someone shoot Churchill?" He simply expected that violence had ended this statesman's life. Television, in performing its legitimate role of bringing us news of the world, has left us somewhat immune to the impact of violence. In the late 1980s we had a problem when one of our students was hurt in a fight with some boys from another school. Despite comments from school leaders about the fact that we hope students would not act like the Irish or Arab extremists, only a tough policy by the school kept some of the boys from seeking revenge. They apparently had learned little or nothing from the cycles of attack and retaliation they saw endlessly and tragically repeated on the evening news.

It is revealing that I hear far less talk among today's students than their predecessors about the nuclear dilemma. They do not appear to find the possibility of nuclear annihilation of all life a factor influencing their thought or behavior. Earlier generations did. Is the change because today's students have come to believe that if we have lived for forty years without nuclear war, then we can avoid the holocaust throughout their lifetime? Or is it because the news they watch gives it so little attention? Of course, the news does report disarmament negotiations, but so far they have only been reductions in overkill, not an elimination of the possibility of all of mankind's death. The news gives much more attention to the fate of a handful of hostages than to the potential but not actual destruction of millions of lives. Or is it because this generation has chosen to avoid thinking about what so many of us have called "the unthinkable"? Or is it because students do realize the complexity of this issue and prefer to leave the solution to experts? Whatever the reason for this situation, it is instructive that this generation of young people appears to be uninvolved in the issue that could most totally alter life as we know it.

Television news must dramatically limit the time allocated to any serious issue. Similarly, comedy or dramatic shows have thirty to sixty minutes, minus a considerable amount of time for commercials, to state a problem in human relationships, struggle with it, and finally, resolve it. Here is one case where the "soaps" may be more realistic. Problems are never resolved the same day they are introduced. But for almost every other show, the problem must be solved just before the final credits come on. Although our youngsters understand that these problems are fiction and not reality, the constant repetition of problems in human relationships being resolved so quickly must have an effect on them as they seek to work out their own relationships. If the relationship cannot be quickly corrected, go on to another one.

This leads us to another way in which the repetitive effect of television deeply touches our children. If acts of physical violence are shown too often, verbal violence is repeated incessantly. One need only watch any situation comedy. During a half-hour show, a derogatory or smart-aleck remark will be made twenty to forty times. Each time, the remark is greeted with a burst of canned laughter. In a year of watching, how many times will a child learn the lesson that saying something insulting at someone else's expense will earn laughter and approval? How difficult it is for parents or teachers to help students develop respect and consideration for others when the opposite behavior is constantly being reinforced in very positive ways.

The fourth influence of visual media also affects how people will treat each other. Until recently television stayed clear of too much explicit sex. The rating system of movies produced at least some controls over what children watched. With videocassettes and cable television readily available, children have access to a much greater range of sexual material. Whether or not what they watch is explicit, the message is clear: sexual behavior is appropriate whenever two persons, of whatever gender, find each other attractive. If after a sexual encounter some mutual concern or even a form of emotional bonding occurs, that is nice. But commitment grows from sexual activity, rather than sexual activity being an expression of commitment. There is, however, one form of sexual conduct that is almost never shown in movies or on television: sex between a married couple. What traditional values hold to be normative is in the media so rare as to be almost unmentionable.

Thus far we have been looking at the effects of the amount of time spent watching and the content of the programs watched. Educators are just now beginning to give attention also to how watching programs or playing video games affects mental ability. In the *Harvard Education Letter* of March 1990, Patricia Marks Greenfield writes:

"The video screen is helping children develop a new kind of literacy—visual literacy—that they will need to thrive in a technological world. In television or film, the viewer must mentally integrate diverse camera shots of a scene to construct an image of the whole. This is an element of visual literacy: an understanding of the code by which to interpret linkage between shots or views."[2]

She goes on to say that video games train youngsters for a different kind of linkage. She cites a study of children in southern California which indicates that 94 percent of children say they have played video games either at home or in an arcade. In most video games, different scenes are linked usually with stairways or doorways. In order to become skilled, players must put individual scenes together in their minds to form a map of its layout. The same sort of mapping of links is necessary to understand computer programming. Greenfield says: "A video game provides informal education that is relevant to the world of computers."[3] She summarizes her findings:

"The dynamic visual imagery shared by film and all of the video media produces a number of cognitive benefits: (1) an array of visual literacy skills, (2) better acquisition of information in general, and (3) better acquisition of action information in particular. On the negative side, dynamic visual imagery leads to (1) decreased stimulation of the imagination, (2) a decrease in mental effort, and (3) a decrease in attention to purely verbal information."[4]

Families

Most young people spend more hours in front of a television set than they do in meaningful interaction with other members of their family. But the influences provided by the media are fairly similar for all young people. It is the family that is most likely to shape the individual characteristics of each child. The family structure in America has been changing for many years. In some ways families of the students of the 1990s are not unique. But trends that have been developing for decades are now certainties. Before the development of modern medicine, infant and child mortality meant that most people could expect to lose a sibling or two, and many people lost a parent before they were adults. Even if the death of a family member did not happen, every individual had to grow up with the knowledge that it was a real possibility. Today such deaths are rare, but every child has to grow up with a different possibility—the divorce of his or her parents. Even among those schoolchildren who expect to go to college, each day one out of every five goes home to just one adult. One out of every two children will spend some part of his or her childhood living with just one adult.

Several points need to be made about the effect of the high divorce rate on American children. First, all of us who are educators have known children of divorce who are very well adjusted and highly successful. Children react to divorce in a variety of ways. However, I believe that the general climate of divorce, the particular effect on some children, and the possibility for all children, are important factors in the lives of the students in the 1990s. I am not surprised that the most troubled class I have known as a headmaster had twice as many single-parent families as the average for the whole school.

Second, death is rarely a matter of choice. Divorce is almost always deliberate for at least one of the partners. Thus, the sense of being "deserted" and the feelings of guilt or anger are likely to be much greater with divorce.

Third, children of divorced parents are more likely to learn to be adaptable and this is a useful skill in an ever-changing world. They often have to adjust to step-parents or step-siblings. In cases of joint custody or even visitation rights, they have to learn to meet alternating situations and different styles of parenting.

Fourth, an environment in which so many people break the vows and commitments involved in marriage (and most people still want the traditional forms of a ceremony that includes vows) teaches children a strong lesson about promises. They see that such things may be important, but they are not binding. Thus, the concept of one's word being one's bond is seen to be inappropriate when one's long-range self-satisfaction and self-fulfillment are at stake.

Finally, the divorce rate has an impact on schools. While some children of divorce are emotionally stable and very accomplished, many are not. Schools have to serve the needs of children who are coping with the sense of loss, guilt, or anger that divorce sometimes brings. Similarly, schools must deal with parents who may be carrying guilt and anger toward the opposite sex or whose emotional lives and sense of worth are all tied up in their children because they have no significant adult in their lives. Furthermore, there is a demand from parents that the school assume ever greater responsibilities that used to be assigned to them. These demands, of course, may also come from parents who are married but who both have careers and, therefore, less time for parenting. Requests for after-school care and weekend programs have increased and will grow during the 1990s. So will insistence on teaching of subjects that traditionally were handled by parents. These include sex, drug, and health education, money management, career counseling, and value formation. The amount of money, time, and human resources devoted to these topics must inevitably detract from resources spent on academic matters. Yet the weakening of the family structure in America makes educators feel that for the welfare of their students, they must give considerable attention to these subjects.

Even for those 50 percent of children whose parents do not divorce, other trends are dramatically shaping their lives. The number of working mothers has increased tremendously in the last generation. Many of the mothers of college-bound students are now pursuing professional careers. These careers, of course, are even more demanding on time and travel than the occupations traditionally held by women in the past. Moreover, professional families are less likely to settle in the geographic region they came from and more likely to make more geographic moves in the course of a lifetime. This means that just at the time when the nuclear family is less stable than ever before in our history, young people are likely to grow up geographically removed from the extended family of grandparents and aunts and uncles. Changing locations for a parent's career may mean that a child has less sense of a permanent community that might have provided some supports no longer supplied by the nuclear or extended family.

Sometimes I am quite struck with the sensitivity of students to family matters. When our youngest son was born shortly after I became headmaster, our boarding students hung a sign that covered several dormitory windows: "Welcome, Kevin." Of course, it had no meaning to him, but it certainly pleased his parents. Even more impressive were the two boys who came to the house a week later. They had presents for my two older children and explained: "We know that the baby is getting a lot of presents. We think your older children may be feeling neglected." No adult had thought of that, and it was all the more sensitive because both of these boys were the youngest ones in their own families.

Social Life

Watching television, even with others present in the room, is basically an individual activity. It does not develop human relationships. The changes in family life, of both the nuclear and the extended family, also lead to a sense of isolation and aloneness for today's students. These factors, in turn, have influenced their social lives. Today's adolescents are very much groupies; apparently they are happiest in large gatherings. While teenagers have always liked to hang out together, the style of the late 1980s was for literally hundreds of high school students to gather at one place. In urban areas, even the idea of having a school dance holds little appeal. Four or five neighboring schools have to be invited or, better yet, the party should be an "open" one, to which anyone may come. The idea of being invited anywhere has almost disappeared. Young people simply find out where the largest open party is being held and arrive there. What is the appeal of the large, open party? That there will be a greater opportunity to meet more people? That at such a mass gathering, one loses the sense of individual responsibility, as people often do in a crowd, and can behave however one wants? Or is it that to issue invitations is to be exclusive, to have to decide for some people and against others, and that would be tantamount to making a judgment? Perhaps it is a combination of all three motives.

Another significant feature of the social scene is that it is very unusual for plans to be made in advance. I see my own children, having spent all week in school with their friends, making and receiving five to ten phone calls on a Friday evening before reaching a decision about what to do that night. Is this because making plans is to make a commitment? Is it hard for them to take the initiative after so much passive entertainment? Or is it simply the need to be sure that one only goes "where the action is"?

Not surprising for the children of the moon, relationships with the opposite sex tend to be intense and yet brief. There is a search for high emotion, yet an unwillingness or an inability for most teenagers to maintain relationships for more than a few months.

One aspect of adolescent social life that I find very encouraging is that they are often able to maintain friendships with persons of the opposite sex with whom they are not romantically involved. This was less true for those who grew up between World War II and Vietnam. Being able to treat people as friends and not as romantic partners is an important attribute in children of the 1990s and will be even more important to them as they enter a working world that is still struggling with the role of women.

In the 1990s there is one fact that overshadows many other aspects of social life, and that is the growing threat of AIDS. If the epidemic spreads to the general population, as many experts believe it will, the effect on our young people will be dramatic. I belong to the last generation that grew up "before the party began." Fear of pregnancy, old moral taboos, and the strong disapproval of authority figures all combined to influence our sexual behavior. Certainly these factors did not prevent premarital sex, but they made it something that had to be done in secret, often in fear and guilt. The pill, the legalization of abortion, and the demand for freedom of the late 1960s produced the sexual revolution. The university is the highest symbol of America's regard for its young people. Until the early 1960s universities were suspending or expelling students for violating sexual norms or even for being in the wrong place at the wrong time. Within a few years coeducational dormitories were the norm; universities made no attempt to be *in loco parentis* in sexual matters, and even real parents turned a blind eye to much sexual behavior.

Because of AIDS, it is quite likely that for the children of the moon, the party is now over. If the disease becomes an epidemic, those who practice sexual freedom will die. They will not die immediately, but as more and more "people like us" contract AIDS, there will inevitably be a change in sexual practices and attitudes. It is too soon to say what shape it will take, but there will be change.

College-bound high school students have already shown that after some delay they will modify their behavior when presented with health information. They smoke tobacco at a significantly lower rate than their contemporaries who are not planning to attend college. Inevitably the threat of AIDS will influence their behavior.

Both the social scene and sexual activity depend on heavy use of alcohol. On December 31, 1989, the lead article of *The Washington Post*'s Outlook section was written by Patrick Welsh, a teacher at an Alexandria, Virginia, high school. It was entitled "Kids and Booze." Mr. Welsh points out that high school students in other generations have been drinking, but he says: "What's new is how young they start, the amount they drink, and how fast they drink it." He quotes Richard Schwartz, Clinical Professor of Pediatrics at Georgetown Medical School: "The main difference is that many of these kids go to a party with the intention of getting drunk. They drink unbelievably large volumes of alcohol in a very short period of time. They have apparatuses like beer bongs, and competitive drinking games to increase the volume and rapidity of ingestion." A letter in response to Mr. Welsh's article pointed out that the pressures of college admissions cannot be blamed for the heavy drinking. It said:. "In 1988 a national survey by the Center for Disease Control reported that 20% of eighth graders have used alcohol in the past month, and 12.5% had five or more drinks on at least one occasion during the preceeding two weeks."

Interestingly, the increased use of alcohol appears to be the negative side of a decrease in drug use. On February 14, 1990, *The New York Times* published the results of a confidential survey of high school seniors by the Institute of Social Research of the University of Michigan. At the end of the 1970s almost 40 percent of high school students said they had used one or more illicit drugs in the last thirty days. By the end of the '80s, that number had fallen below 20 percent. The article quoted Secretary of Health and Human Services Louis W. Sullivan: "It is obvious from these survey findings that young people have made dramatic changes in their own use of most illicit drugs, as well as changes in their attitudes toward drug use by others during the decade of the 1980s."

For college-bound students at the start of the last decade of the century, alcohol is clearly the drug of choice. They do appear to have a desire to limit its most dangerous effects. Many high schools have chapters of Students Against Drunk Driving and the practice of having a designated driver at parties is growing. However, American adolescents follow their parents in the belief that artificial mood control is acceptable behavior, and at times they appear to consider it almost a God-given right.

Other Trends

One of the best ways to predict the behavior of secondary school students is to observe the behavior of college students. One might think that certain types of behavior would be developed in high school and then taken to college. In fact, the reverse seems to be more often the case—secondary school students two or three years later emulating the behavior of college students. Sometimes these are merely fads. In the mid-'80s baseball caps became very popular among college males. By the late '80s, high school administrators were beginning to pass rules against wearing baseball caps in hallways and classrooms. More often the imitation of collegiate behavior is of a serious nature. The problems of alcohol and attendant misbehavior are rampant on college campuses and, not surprisingly, copied by high school students.

Colleges are now moving away from the laissez-faire attitudes about discipline that existed from the early '70s onward. In April of 1990 *Time* magazine ran an article entitled "Waging War on the Greeks: Fraternities and Sororities Are Being Forced to Clean Up Their Acts." The same month *The Washington Post* reported:

"Campus life is deteriorating, particularly at large universities, according to a report released yesterday that said college officials should re-emphasize 'enduring values' of academia to curb offensive behavior that includes alcohol abuse, crime, and intolerance. The one-year study released yesterday by the Carnegie Foundation for the Advancement of Teaching attributes deterioration partly to the abandonment by colleges of the traditional role as substitute parents. In the survey of college presidents, 52% said the quality of campus life was more of a concern than it was a few years ago. They most frequently identified substance abuse, primarily alcohol, as their biggest concern, followed by student apathy and crime."[5]

Clearly, the same problems that worry college administrators concern those of us in secondary schools. Recently, the heads of seven independent schools in the Washington area signed a letter that was sent to all the parents of their schools. Because it addresses important social problems, I quote it in its entirety on pages 33 and 34.

Another disturbing phenomenon appears to be moving from the college to secondary school students. Adolescent boys have always wished for more impressive bodies. Many of us can remember reading with interest the Charles Atlas ads in comic books. But at this time the emphasis on weight training for athletes, combined with the availability of steroids, is creating a dangerous situation for students.

St. Albans School

Mount St. Alban
Washington, D.C. 20016

Headmaster's Study February 1, 1990

Dear Parents:

We, the heads of seven Washington area schools, take the unusual step of writing a joint letter because of our deep concern about your children. It is clear that many of them are practicing a duality that is morally unhealthy and potentially very dangerous. Our students are bright, hard working, and full of promise. In our schools they are generally responsible citizens. Yet many of them act on weekends with an entirely different set of principles. On most weekends in the Washington area when students from our schools tend to socialize together, there is at least one, and sometimes several, large teenage parties. They are frequently "open," meaning that anyone feels that he or she has a right to attend. Sometimes several hundred adolescents attend one party. There is often little or no adult supervision. Excessive drinking and sexual license are common. Destruction of property and fighting are not infrequent. It would be hard to devise a better recipe for disaster than a social scene that includes the anonymity provided by an "open party," no adult supervision, considerable amounts of alcohol, and teenage hormones which encourage sexual or violent behavior.

Young people cannot be allowed to believe that behavior which is totally unacceptable at our schools will be tolerated off campus. All of us, parents and teachers, need to make it clear that we expect the same sense of responsibility, self-discipline, and respect for others and their property off campus as we do on campus.

This is a problem which affects students at all our schools. While our schools cannot assume parental responsibility for off campus behavior, we will make it clear to our students that we will respond to improper and irresponsible behavior, whether it happens on or off campus. Not to do so would be to allow a few individuals to bring disrepute to a school and thus hurt all its students. Most important, it would teach young people that a dual morality is acceptable. We will continue our efforts to provide moral education for our students with particular attention to matters of alcohol, drugs, and sexuality.

Page 2

We urge parents to accept their responsibilities for the behavior of their children out of school. You can do this in a number of ways:

(1) making it clear that no party is to be held in your home when you are not present;

(2) providing active supervision if you agree to have a party in your home;

(3) insisting that your children not attend a party when they do not know the host family and reminding them that they must leave a party if asked to do so by the host;

(4) reminding them that decent, responsible behavior is not an "on" and "off" matter, but something to be expected at all times.

The party scene as it now exists in the Washington area not only puts adolescents at considerable physical risk, but also condones and encourages irresponsible and improper behavior. All of us who care for our young people must do all that we can to encourage, even insist, that at all times they act in a way that reflects what is best in them and will help them to grow into men and women of good character.

Sincerely,

Robert C. Barry
Georgetown Preparatory School

Malcolm Coates
Landon School

Joseph J. Ciancaglini
Gonzaga College High School

Agnes C. Underwood
National Cathedral School

Charles P. Lord
Holton-Arms School

Mark H. Mullin
St. Albans School

Earl G. Harrison, Jr.
Sidwell Friends School

Apparently the problem is widespread enough that in May 1990, the University of Maryland advertised a free symposium on steroids, open to all high school students in the Washington area. The principal speaker was a former professional football player who was awaiting a heart transplant because his own heart was ruined by steroid use.

Sometimes the imitation of college students by their younger brothers and sisters has beneficial effects. The interest in the environment which is an important movement on many college campuses has now caught the fancy of secondary school students. Ecology groups are appearing at both high schools and elementary schools. It was not atypical that recently the students of an elementary school in the Washington area purchased ten acres of South American rain forests to be held in perpetuity. Generally it has been students who have pushed faculty and administrators to develop recycling programs within schools. I even know of one group of students who offered to buy and wash each day ceramic mugs for each faculty member to phase out the use of styrofoam cups for coffee.

The emphasis on social services seen on many college campuses is frequently mirrored at secondary schools. Students express their desire to be of help to others in a wide variety of ways. They are prepared to respond to dramatic problems. After the 1989 hurricane in South Carolina, a consortium of schools in the Washington area sent a busload of students to help with the clean-up. Sometimes a service is on a very individual basis. I know of one student who spends one afternoon a week reading aloud to an elderly widow.

Frequently the social service experience brings out a sensitivity in a young person that is truly remarkable. I am pleased to quote Jacob Montwieler, a high school student who worked as a volunteer at the Vietnam Memorial, on his reaction to the experience.

"Last August, that dreadful month when the temperature and the humidity soar to the intolerable heights so that one often longs for a quiet air-conditioned classroom, I volunteered at the Vietnam Veterans Memorial, working from the cool hours of the morning into the hot hours of the afternoon, when only the most diligent of tourists are out. While my other classmates worked in the white-walled, immaculate rooms of hospitals or nursing homes I fulfilled my social service requirement at The Wall where I had to battle the infamous weather of Washington as well as the hordes of tourists that come every summer to find the names of deceased friends and relatives. Every day at The Wall I found that there were names without faces, and faces without names. But gradually, the two began to merge.

"I had been working there for a week and had moved into a pretty routine schedule. The sun beat down as relentlessly as ever that Friday, and when two o'clock came around I was looking forward to a relaxing weekend at the beach. I was standing at my usual post at the end of the monument when an attractive middle-aged woman with shoulder-length curly brown hair approached me. She was wearing light blue pants and a light green blouse. Very pastel, I thought, as I noticed the rose-tinted glasses that hid her eyes.

" 'Are you a volunteer?' she asked.

"I smiled and took off my National Park Service baseball cap. I gave it a flourish and replied, 'Yes, ma'am, what can I do for you?'

" 'I'm looking for a name,' she replied in a soft voice. She seemed uncertain so I offered to find the name for her.

" 'It's Jerold Wilson,' she said. 'He died on May 17, 1969.' I looked up his name in the book and began to walk down the stone path. I stopped for a minute to make sure she was following me and put my hat on backwards so it held my bangs, which often fell into my eyes. She must have been a newlywed, I thought, and I cringed.

"I smiled and told her a little bit about the monument. When we reached the correct panel, I pointed his name out. It was four lines from the top on one of the taller panels. She looked up towards the top and placed her hand on top of her glasses so she could afford a better look.

" 'If you like I can make a rubbing onto a piece of paper for you.'

"She turned around to look at me. 'Um, sure. Thanks a lot.'

" 'It will just take a second,' I said and quickly walked up the hill to the kiosk. A minute later I walked back down, ladder wedged between my arm and chest. I put the stepladder down and climbed to the top with a pencil and a piece of paper. When I touched the black granite surface, it burned my fingers, and I yelped, nearly falling off the ladder. Hoping for a sympathetic look, I turned around, but the lady's eyes did not stray.

"The monument was burning as I centered the piece of paper on his name. I switched hands and started to make a rubbing for her. My fingertips burned as if I held a hot lump of coal in my hand, and I was angry at the widow for making me do this. I glanced under my arm. She had taken her glasses off, and was dabbing her eyes with a handkerchief. I sighed, partly annoyed and partly sympathetic, but I put a smile on my face as I climbed down the ladder.

"The rubbing held loosely between my thumb and first two fingers, I approached her and saw her large eyes were glazed with tears. Trying to sound happy I spoke to her in a soft voice, 'Here you go.'

"She didn't move and I repeated my words in a louder voice, 'Here's your rubbing.' I reached out my hand and she took it. My first impulse was to draw back but I held on as the sheet fell to the ground. She laced her fingers with mine and clenched my hand. We made eye contact for the first time as she spoke, 'He was my brother.' I stood dumbfounded and tried to think of something to say.

"She squeezed my hand, and for a moment I was her brother, saying goodbye for the last time.

"At that moment I saw a different side of the war. It was not pity for the young soldiers who died, or anger at their deaths. Rather, it was sympathy for their friends and relatives who lived each day with part of their lives missing. I knew then that part of them had died in Vietnam too. I realized then how great was the power of love. I had felt her love flow to her fingertips and go into me. Because she had taken this trip to Washington, because she came to The Wall and asked me—the only young male volunteer—for help, because she had held my hand, but most importantly, because she loved her brother, I loved him too."

Colleges have also seen a growing interest in religion, a trend which is occasionally present in the secondary schools. A few years ago, one of our students was badly hurt in an automobile accident and was immobilized in a hospital bed. Several of his classmates came to me and asked if I would put my name on the prayer wheel. I replied, "What prayer wheel?" They showed me a large pie-shaped drawing divided into twenty-four segments, one for each hour of the day. Many of the segments had a name written in it. The students explained that they would tape it to the ceiling above the injured boy's bed so that any time of day or night he woke up in pain, he could look at the wheel to see the name of someone who had promised to pray for him at that hour.

Unfortunately, recent reports have indicated that racial and religious tolerance is being threatened on some college campuses. Verbal abuse and offensive signs have begun to appear with enough regularity to be frightening. The spring 1990 issue of the *Harvard Alumni Magazine* reported that the university is wrestling with the issue of how far to go in permitting free speech while discouraging racially and religiously offensive comments. I am not aware that these issues have appeared at secondary schools yet. It would be an unwise secondary school administrator, however, who assumes that this particular problem of the college campus will not come to his or her school. In general, I would say that the emerging student generation appears to be moving at about the same pace as the society as a whole in its attitude toward those who have been discriminated against in the past.

In matters of race, secondary students' attitudes are very much in the American mainstream at the end of the century. They are rigorously opposed to overt racism, particularly when it is far away as in South Africa. They are uncertain and ambivalent about attempts to redress previous social unbalance by affirmative action. They occasionally make racial remarks or jokes in private. In social matters they are relatively color-blind in their friendships. Interracial dating is accepted in many areas of the country, but few are ready for interracial marriage.

Similarly, the majority of students are moving at the same pace as the rest of society on gender issues. They are opposed to overt discrimination; they are aware that for both economic security and personal fulfillment most college-educated women will want careers. Young women believe it is possible to have both a career and children, but they recognize it is very demanding. Moreover, many women are ambivalent about whether they should be equal breadwinners with their husbands or whether he should be the major source of income for the family. Male students believe the women should have equal rights, but often harbor a feeling of male superiority and the belief that there are still roles and actions that are traditionally male or female. A woman biology teacher told me recently that her tenth grade students were dissecting a fetal pig. She overheard one boy say to another: "Oh, go ahead, touch it. Don't be a girl." She realized that the remark had just slipped out. Of course, she pointed out to the embarrassed boy that she, who did all sorts of dissections, had caught him in his chauvinism.

Economics

There are two economic realities that must be considered when thinking about the students of the 1990s and their families. The first has been true for most American teenagers for several generations, but it is still important: when youngsters grew up on farms, by the time they were in their early teens they were able to make important contributions to the family's economic welfare. This was even more true on the less mechanized labor-intensive farms of past generations. By contrast, today's young people in urban and suburban America are a very serious financial drain on a family. If they go to college or, worse yet, graduate school, they will be a burden even after they have legally become adults. What money they may earn may help pay some of their expenses, but is almost never enough to meet all expenses, much less contribute to the rest of the family. It must have been very different to know that even as a teenager one could and should contribute significantly to the family instead of the opposite experience of being a financial drain until one is well into one's twenties. Human beings enjoy the feeling of being needed, of contributing to the welfare of others. However, except for contrived chores, this feeling is largely denied to American college-bound students. Schools would do well to consider finding significant ways that students can contribute to other people. Many schools do offer opportunities for social service.

While students do not contribute to the economic welfare of their families, many schools report a considerable increase in the number of students who have after-school jobs. This employment does not help the family, but usually provides the pocket money needed to keep the record, clothing, and fast-food industries happy. For some students, the experience of a paying job is a very valuable one, but for others, it means that school and studying become increasingly secondary activities in their lives.

A second economic factor appears to have become a condition of life in America during the last two decades of the century. The American dream has always been for each generation to achieve greater success than the one before it. The poor immigrant son who attained wealth or fame through education and hard work was more than a legend. For many families it was a reality. And it was true until recently that, except for the children of the very rich, young people could look forward to greater material prosperity than their parents had enjoyed. However, the inflation of the 1970s, and the slipping of America as the dominant force in international economics, have changed that. At a time when for a variety of reasons we have a generation that seems less patient than those that went before it, there is a real possibility that many of them will not reach or surpass the level of economic well-being achieved by their parents. Inevitably, this causes frustration and anxiety. It is always difficult to accept a reduction in the standard of living, and students who worry about this possibility are not being unrealistic. In a society in which so many persons measure their self-worth by their material possessions, this is particularly threatening. Unless there is a major change in the economy of the United

States, even those who receive a college education cannot be sure of attaining the material rewards their parents had.

Those of us who work in schools in Washington, D.C. see the same phenomenon in a different dimension. Washington has many teenagers whose parents have been highly successful elsewhere, and then come into positions of power and prominence in Washington. Yet the realistic child knows that he or she will almost inevitably attain less fame and national influence than the parent. It is a very rare senator's child who can expect to exceed the accomplishment of his or her parent. The child knows this from a young age. For many this causes anxiety and sometimes neurosis.

What is true in terms of prestige and power for the children of the politically successful in Washington is increasingly true for more and more children of the middle class in all of America. This naturally adds to the competitive pressures on our students and to their anxieties about their futures and their self-worth. The possibility that they will not achieve the American dream of continued progress is one of the most important factors shaping the students of the 1990s and making them different from the generations that have gone before them.

Other Attributes

Two other qualities occur to me as I think of my students. Most of them are fun to be with. They know how to tease adults in a humorous and effective way. They can even laugh at themselves. I have frequently had difficulty getting the seniors to maintain the Senior Room at any level above total disaster. For some reason, the room that belongs to them is the one in which they want to make the largest mess. Recently, in utter frustration, I announced that I would close and padlock the room. An hour later, three boys came to me and said: "Will you please come with us? We want to show you something." I had a pretty good idea we were headed for a cleaned-up Senior Room. Not only was all the mess gone, but a quick coat of paint had been applied to the walls. The final touch, however, was that instead of their usual rock music blaring from a stereo, the gentle strains of Beethoven greeted me as I entered the room. Of course, the padlock was never applied.

We also had a problem with senior pranks carried out a week or two before graduation. I finally outlawed them and threatened the diploma of any boy who participated in a prank. That spring all was quiet and peaceful. Graduation day arrived and I thought I had won the battle. However, as each boy received his diploma from me, he handed me three jelly beans. Now a headmaster can handle a few jelly beans at graduation, but when he is in a graduation gown with no pockets, and it is a warm June day, causing the jelly beans to begin to melt, he is soon in trouble. I looked for places to put them. Soon I was dropping them and they began to bounce on the floor. The seniors received their diplomas and won the last victory over the headmaster. The next year, I was in even more trouble as each graduate received his diploma and handed me an egg. Fortunately, I never found out whether they were cooked or uncooked.

My students even seem to know when to take the headmaster seriously and when to ignore him. One day, a few days before our final football game of the season, we arrived at school to find that there had been a visit from the opposing school. Its name was written in bright letters on the sidewalks around our school, and even down the side of a stone cross. I am quite sure that the perpetrators had not intended to deface a cross; they simply had not realized what it was in the dark night when they brought their paint. I called the headmaster of the other school and told him that we could clean up the sidewalks, but I was going to leave the name of his school written on the side of the stone cross. Then people who were thinking about whether to send their son to his school or mine could get an idea of what sorts of students he had. He gagged once and said: "I do not know who they are but I will be there in an hour with the culprits." Indeed, he was. However, when I told my students that they must not make fun of their rivals who were on their hands and knees scrubbing away the paint in front of our school, my command fell on deaf ears. The midnight painters had damaged egos as well as sore knees.

I am also impressed with the sense of fairness of today's students. Most of them know that when they have done something wrong, fairness requires a response from the school. I remember one young man whom I had to suspend in a rather controversial case. How touched I was some years later when he asked me to participate in his commissioning as an officer in the U.S. Marine Corps. He said: "I was mad at you when you punished me, but I knew then and I am even more certain now that what you did was in my best interest because it helped me get on the right path." This sense of fairness makes our students able to understand another's point of view.

Today's students do not always immediately understand others, but more than many of their predecessors, they have an ability to be open-minded when something is pointed out to them. They are basically of goodwill. Best of all, it has been my experience that although they will occasionally act in ways I would not choose for them, when a serious request is made of them and they understand the reason for it, they respond magnanimously and cooperatively. Teaching and working with them is rewarding because they are well intentioned.

We have seen that the children of the moon are more sophisticated than earlier generations. They are more adaptable and able to handle change. Their lives are very much shaped by constant exposure to television. If they do not feel as threatened by the possibility of nuclear annihilation as their parents did, they also face three very serious threats. Even the chance that one of these threats might become an individual reality shapes both their emotional state and their behavior. The threats are, of course, AIDS, divorce (either of their parents or of themselves), and economic uncertainty. Having looked at some of the characteristics of the students of the 1990s, we are now ready to consider the role of their parents.

Chapter Three

The Hearts of Parents

I would like now to give some thought to those who are most influential in the lives of children, their parents. Parenting has always been one of the most difficult of human activities. Most of the training we receive is from observing our own parents firsthand or other parents secondhand. All of us bring to our own parenting a mixture of imitating and reacting against the examples we have experienced. Until one has been a parent, it is impossible to understand how much a parent loves a child and how vulnerable a parent is through his or her children. In fact, that is the one thing that none of us, parents or teachers, can teach our children: how much we love them. Only when they have their own children will they understand that.

Because of the force of this love, it is difficult for those of us who are parents to be objective about our children. It is even harder for us always to practice what is best for them. As I write about parenting, I am acutely aware of the weaknesses I have as a parent. I know there have often been times when I have not met my own children's needs.

I find the parents I work with terribly concerned about their children, eager to do the right thing and willing to make great sacrifices for them. They want what is best for their children and seek to give them the right opportunities to build productive and happy lives. I am also pleased that parents often express appreciation for the men and women who teach their children. For example, several hundred parents at my school give tremendously of their time to produce a Christmas House Tour that raises money for cash grants for teachers.

I am always touched when families who are making a sacrifice to pay tuition also choose to make a gift to the school. I am even more impressed when parents and past parents are willing to serve as fund-raisers and ask their friends to contribute. Many parents respond most generously and they occasionally respond with great humor.

Two of our parents went to call on a St. Albans family. When the husband showed them into the living room, they were horrified to see his wife sitting in an easy chair covered with bandages, her left arm and right leg tucked out of sight behind her. The callers gasped, "What on earth happened?" She laughed as she stood up and dropped the bandages. "I knew you would want me to give an arm and a leg for St. Albans." I am happy to say that she and her husband did make a very generous pledge to the school.

Parents help in other ways; they also share in the difficulties that all of us, teachers and parents, have in communicating with the young. I remember one mother who knew both my wife and me well. When she called me at the office, I could hear amusement in her voice. She said: "I want to congratulate you. My nine-year-old son came home today and announced that the Headmaster is getting married on Saturday." I was puzzled for a second, and then remembered that earlier in the day I had been talking to the boys about the importance of chapel in the life of the alumni. I said that many of them come back for weddings, baptisms, and funerals. Sometimes even their relatives use the chapel for special events. I told the boys that on the next Saturday, I would be marrying the daughter of an alumnus in the chapel. The nine-year-old had taken me quite literally.

Of course, the most important way a parent shows appreciation to teachers is with a simple thank you and words of praise. Teachers receive small financial rewards and frequently get very little recognition. A note or phone call from a parent about something the teacher has done well does so much to lift the morale of an educator.

I cannot resist telling of the time when I most impressed a group of parents. I was Assistant Headmaster of the Blue Ridge School. At one parent gathering I announced that we really believed we were good at teaching and that we could teach anybody anything. At that, the Athletic Director came on stage with a golden retriever. I asked the dog, "What is two plus two?" He barked four times and happily trotted over to the Athletic Director to receive a milk bone. "What is three minus one?" There were two barks and the dog received another milk bone. "Let's get really hard. What is the square root of twenty-five?" I was rewarded with five barks and the dog got yet another milk bone. I invited the parents to ask math questions from the floor, and to their continued amazement, the dog got all the answers correct. I think very few of them realized that the Athletic Director had trained his pet to bark rhythmically while he held his hand upside down with a milk bone in it, and to stop barking when he turned his hand over and prepared to deliver the milk bone. I had no worries about the dog, but I was concerned that we would get a question that the Athletic Director could not handle.

Influence of the 1960s

Just as young people reflect the times in which they live, parents do also. We need to consider not only how the attitudes and expectations of today's parents affect children, but also how these parents interact with teachers and schools. What distinctive characteristics mark those who bore and are raising the children of the moon?

Obviously, the ages of the parents in a particular grade of children will vary greatly, depending on when the parents began having children and what position among siblings a child holds. Moreover, the increase in divorce, remarriage, and second families in our society further expands the age span of a group of parents. However, the vast majority of those who will have children in secondary school during the 1990s will, themselves, have been in either high school or college between 1966 and 1973. While few of them will have been particularly active in "the movement" or gone to extremes with alternative lifestyles, all of them will have been influenced to some degree by the strong cultural forces that swept this country in the late 1960s. It is important for educators to recognize this as they interact with parents. It is also important for parents to realize how they may have been influenced in their formative years as they seek to guide their children through the same period of development.

There are at least eight characteristics of the 1960s worth our consideration. It is dangerous to generalize and suppose that every parent will have been touched equally by all eight factors. But it would be equally unwise to imagine that there will be many parents in the 1990s whose own lives were not changed in some way.

First, the 1960s helped us understand that external appearance is not as important as was once believed. While extremes of dress or hair may indicate significant extremes in attitude or philosophy, they may be mere adolescent experimentation or conformity to peer expectations.

Many of those whose hair or clothing troubled their parents during the 1960s were actually traditional in their long-range goals. The knowledge that this is the case helped many parents and educators be relatively relaxed as a number of youngsters in the 1980s experimented with the "punk" style. I remember when the first boy showed up at my school in 1984 with dyed hair and an earring. A week went by and no one said anything to him about it. Finally, he could not stand it any longer, came into my office, and said, "Well, what do you think?" I answered with all the innocence I could muster, "Think about what?" The look of total dejection on his face made me realize it may have been one of the cruelest things I have said to a student.

A second aspect of the 1960s was the widespread belief that everyone had the right to question authority. Corollary to this was the notion that the "expert" or "professional" is likely to be obstinate or arrogant or lacking common sense or just plain wrong. Therefore, one needed to challenge or be suspicious of people who claim that their training or experience gives them special knowledge. Of course, this can run the democratic ideal to the extreme. It is one thing to say that all people are equal in the eyes of God or the eyes of the law. It is quite another to say that all are equal in knowledge or experience. This attitude, even though rarely expressed so baldly, influences the way some parents respond to teachers. Now more than ever before in our history, some parents show little respect for teachers. This is impossible to hide from children and thus robs teachers of the professionalism they are expected to possess.

A third attitude of the 1960s is that traditions should be continued only if they can be explained and justified within the framework of the ideas, values, and assumptions of the present. They had to be "relevant" or be discarded. The possibility that those who came before us might have had some unique insights into human beings and their needs—and therefore shaped traditions and rituals to meet those needs—was anathema to the view of progress espoused in the 1960s. I found that even in the 1980s younger parents looked at me as though I were slightly deranged when I suggested that some of the traditions at our particular school may have served deep human needs that they had not considered.

This leads to the fourth characteristic, the notion that the young often possess wisdom and a moral sensibility that their elders lack. In a rapidly changing world there may be some truth to the idea that the young are more ready for change, and if we adults appear jaded or cynical there may be some truth to the charge of moral insensibility. But it is folly to assume that those under eighteen are more likely to be correct in matters of judgment or morality than those over thirty. I find that parents who grew up in the 1960s rarely think their children know more than they do, but they often think their children know more than their teachers do.

Democracy is, of course, an essential of American life. Our democratic government has not only made us a great nation, but also given us the invaluable gift of freedom. But a fifth aspect of the 1960s was a desire to carry democracy to an extreme in every area of life. There is an increasing tendency among parents to try to democratize schools. The notion of "the majority" has a sacredness to it that is indeed part of the American experience. I hear parents frequently saying things like "Most of the parents believe . . ." or "Why don't you take a poll to find out what the parents really want?" or "The parents should be able to elect. . . ." Although the question of the correct form of school governance is outside the scope of this work, it is important to see that the demand for greater parental involvement often expressed in terms of the ideal of democracy will continue to grow during the 1990s. Educators will have three choices: (1) accede to such demands, (2) strengthen themselves to resist the demands, or (3) develop new methods for allowing parental involvement without surrendering professional control.

Much of the rhetoric of the 1960s extolled the virtue of freedom. Everyone was to be free "to do his own thing." Yet one of the greatest ironies of the period was that a sense of moral certainty which some possessed actually restricted freedom. The clearest example, of course, was students shouting down speakers whose views of the Vietnam War were not acceptable to them. But it happened in other, more subtle, ways. The force of emotion of the period made dissent from the norm a very difficult thing. I find this attitude lingering in parents who grew up in the era. This brings up the sixth characteristic. When I suggest that one school may do things one way and another school proceed differently, and isn't it good that there are alternatives and choices, I sometimes get a cold response. The parents may have an almost Platonic notion of an "ideal" form for a school, and therefore believe that every school, or at least every one in which they have children, must proceed to imitate that ideal. Even though they are controlled by local school boards, the conformity among public educational institutions in this country is quite amazing. There are many parents who would impose the same conformity among independent schools.

There is one example of this conformity in colleges and universities that is quite striking. Until the 1960s students seeking a college had a choice of attending a coeducational institution or a single-sex college. In the 1960s and early 1970s most people decided that single-sex education was wrong. There are now only a handful of all-male colleges left in the country. Effectively, an American male seeking a college has lost the option of choosing between single-sex education and coeducation. He has fewer alternatives than his father did. Similarly, there has been a reduction in the number of women's colleges. It is interesting, however, that now some of the colleges that remained only for women, such as Wellesley or Bryn Mawr, appear to be doing better than those colleges that previously were single sex and then became coeducational. I will have more to say about gender education in Chapter Seven.

The seventh characteristic, moral indignation, is a particularly unpleasant one. The late 1960s was a period when cooperation and courtesy were in short supply. If one was committed, or even wanted to appear committed, to bringing about the social change that was deemed so necessary, those old niceties were anachronisms for which there simply was not time. Indignation and outrage were the style, and people mocked Lyndon Johnson for saying "Come, let us reason together." Unfortunately, remnants of this attitude can still be found when parents become upset about the education of their youngsters. While most remain civilized in discussions, there are a number who are quick to use offensive (in both senses of the word) language and to show the same indignation and rage that were in vogue when they were students.

Allan Bloom[1] has given us a classic phrase to describe the eighth characteristic of the period. He says that as we moved from the 1950s to the 1960s, "conspicuous compassion replaced conspicuous consumption." He also points out that the emphasis must be placed on "conspicuous." Once the draft was ended and well-educated Americans were not forced to serve in the armed forces, opposition to the Vietnam War was significantly reduced on university campuses, even though the war dragged on for three years. But it would be wrong to think of the 1960s as all hypocrisy and cant. There was a genuine desire to build a better world and much of the anger of the period came from the inevitable frustration when that vision was not realized. While those who were students in the '60s have, as adults, enjoyed returning to the pleasures of consumption, they are still haunted by the appeal to seek the good as they did when they were students. This is reflected in their strong desire that their children be educated morally and in their ability to respond positively when an appeal is made to their own idealism. Both tasks—helping young people grow morally and tapping the idealism of their parents—are important duties of educators in the 1990s.

We have spent some time considering some of the more important trends of the late 1960s. Because these were powerful, the parents of the 1990s were naturally affected by them. Each parent will have been influenced in different ways and to different degrees, but it is important that both parents and educators be aware of the cultural forces that were at work when today's parents were students.

Well-Educated Parents

One thing that is clear about the parents of the 1990s is that they have, as a whole, received more education than any generation before them. To be a college graduate is commonplace, and to have some sort of graduate degree is in no way exceptional. If this is true of the fathers, there has been an even greater change among mothers. The opening of professions to women has meant that more and more young mothers have completed graduate work and are trained in demanding professions. This has three important results. It means that most parents are able to provide a reasonably sophisticated, if not actually intellectual, home environment. Children who are raised by such people who have been educated are exposed to ideas and attitudes that encourage their mental growth. This is the case for the majority of college-bound secondary students.

The high level of parental education raises the possibility that their children will not exceed, and may in fact not even equal, the educational level of their parents. Earlier we saw the same problem about not exceeding the material well-being of their parents. Once again the American dream is of continued progress. *A Nation at Risk* quotes Paul Copperman: "Each generation of Americans has outstripped its parents in education, in literacy, and in economic attainment. For the first time in the history of our country, the educational skills of one generation will not surpass, will not equal, will not even approach those of their parents."[2]

The third effect of high parental education perpetuates and accelerates a trend that has been developing for most of this century. In a society such as the United States before World War I, in which only a few went to college, a teacher with only two years of teachers college had more years of education than the parents of almost all his or her students. Today with many parents having bachelor's degrees and a significant number holding law, business, or other graduate degrees, the secondary teacher—particularly if his or her undergraduate major was in education—will have received significantly less education than the parent with whom the teacher must interact. Teachers have always had to work with parents who had more wealth or power. For secondary teachers to face parents who are better educated, presumably that quality which teachers most value, dramatically changes the dynamics of parent–teacher relationships.

Fast Track Parents

Of course, the higher educational level of parents was attained in order to achieve higher career goals, and this leads us to another characteristic of today's parents. Many are pursuing highly demanding careers and the change has, of course, been greatest among women. While women often work so that the family may maintain a desired standard of living, many of them also want the satisfactions and intangible rewards that come from a successful career. This means that couples, particularly those who want their children to go to college, often postpone having children. Thus, the parents are older when the child is in secondary school. Moreover, the demands of a successful professional, technical, or business career are such that there is less time to spend with children. Time with children decreases exponentially when both parents are in demanding careers. This makes parents anxious and exaggerates the guilt they may feel for the lack of time they are able to give. One response is to put emphasis on "quality time" as opposed to simply being there. Another response is to intervene dramatically, and often inappropriately, when there is a perceived problem. Thus, the parent convinces himself, and tries to convince the child, that he really does care and is involved.

This is an extreme example, but I had one jet-setting lawyer call me at my home three times over one weekend. These calls were made from two different and distant cities. The parent was highly agitated about a disagreement between his fifth grade son and a teacher. Neither discipline nor grades were at issue. This ridiculous situation was further highlighted by the fact that in typical executive style, the upset parent had "gone right to the top," in this case, to the headmaster. He had had neither the courtesy nor the common sense to discuss the matter with the teacher involved and find out what was really going on in the homeroom.

Andree Brooks has written a fascinating book entitled *Children of Fast Track Parents*. She points out that the qualities needed for a successful professional career are often quite different from those needed for successful parenting. Among the qualities she lists as useful in a career are "a constant striving for perfection; mobility; a goal-oriented attitude toward the project at hand; a belief that succeeding must always be the top priority."[3] On the other hand, the good parent has "a tolerance for repeated error; stability; an acceptance of the seemingly capricious nature of child-raising; an understanding that failure promotes growth."[4] In the traditional American family, the father might exemplify the professional qualities while the mother could practice the nurturing ones. In a modern family, both father and mother are expected to develop the professional qualities for their careers and then be able to switch characteristics and exhibit nurturing qualities at home.

Brooks goes on to point out that "control is a major need of many powerful, successful individuals—a characteristic that might be dubbed the King Lear syndrome. Seeing a child become an independent achiever in his or her own right also means a loss of control over that child."[5] Such parents may try not only to control their child, but also to control and manipulate the environment (particularly the school environment) in ways they think will be helpful to their child. Fast track parents are accustomed to keeping score of success, whether that score is measured by financial rewards or by powerful positions. In the same way, there is a natural tendency for such people to keep score with their children. The highest points go to those whose children are admitted to the most selective colleges.

Brooks quotes Dr. David Elkind: "The social pressure on contemporary parents to use their children as symbols of economic surplus and status is powerful, even if parents are not fully aware of it. A successful child is the ultimate proof of one's own success."[6] She goes on to say: "Is there a deeper, more narcissistic motive at work, the idea that admission to an Ivy League college will place the ultimate stamp of approval on one's own accomplishments as a parent? For whether a parent likes it or not, that rejection or acceptance letter becomes a score card. It is as if the parents as well as the child are being evaluated."[7]

It is in contrast to this attitude that Patrick Welsh in *Tales Out of School* quotes Bruno Bettelheim: "The modern, middle-class family still feels that its justification has to be derived from what it produces, but the only thing it produces now are children. Their production should justify the labors, if not the very existence of the family. . . . Perhaps we were all better off when children were seen as a gift of God, however they turned out, and not something the high quality of which provides justification of our family."[8]

Fast track parents are particularly vulnerable to two forms of adolescent reaction. Brooks points out that "high achieving parents should also be prepared for unusually sharp criticism of themselves and their lives from their teenager during adolescence. These youngsters really do have a strong need to unhinge 'perfect' parents as they search for pride in their own identity. For it may be one of the only ways they can bolster their own emerging egos in light of their parents' exceptional achievements. Try not to take it personally."[9] And, of course, parents who view all of life as success or failure, run the risk of encouraging another kind of behavior in their children. Welsh cautions: "A parent who is mainly interested in a child's achievement puts a weapon in that child's hands. That weapon is failure."[10]

A thoughtful and sensitive parent who has achieved much in his or her own life can help young people understand what that achievement means and still inspire them to seek their own accomplishments. One of the best examples I have heard was the address given by the Rev. Jesse Jackson at his son's high school graduation in 1984. At the start of his speech, Mr. Jackson turned slightly to the graduates and said:

"Eighteen years ago I was marching in Selma, Alabama. There was violence and hatred in the streets. I got a message to call home immediately. When I did, I learned that you were born, my son. Eighteen years later you are graduating from one of the finest schools in the land, and I stand before you as a candidate for President of the United States. You will never know, my son, you will never know how far we have come."

Other Concerns

The very high divorce rate of American parents adds to a sense of frustration and guilt for them. Raising a child is hard for two people. It is considerably more difficult for one person, although many single parents carry out the child-raising tasks heroically and successfully. Brooks indicates that the dangers to the child are greatest at the time of the breakup of the marriage. "Virtually all recent students indicate that there is frequently a substantial period of emotional, practical child neglect following parental separation. Much of that neglect appears to come from the personal and economic stress faced by divorcing parents rather than any lack of concern for their youngsters. Children who fare best are those whose parents make specific plans to ensure the continuation of their normal routine, including supervision and discipline."[11] While many parents argue that it is better for a child to be raised in a one-parent home than in a home in which two parents are always fighting, one must also suspect that President Theodore M. Hirshburg of Notre Dame was right when he said: "The most important thing a father can do for his child is to love the child's mother."

If the trends of the 1980s continue, a very significant characteristic of adults in the 1990s will be a growing consumer activism. When applied to schools, this consumerism may have a very salutory effect. Parents are demanding higher standards of teaching and accountability in education. They will put pressure on school boards, administrators, and government officials to make sure that their children are not shortchanged by poor education. The stakes are too high to do otherwise.

On the other hand, when consumer action is applied to individual students, the result may be less beneficial. It is very difficult for a parent to be objective about his or her own child or to see the situation within the broader context of long-range educational goals. Again, to use a silly but true example, a mother of a senior came to see me, expressing her concerns that the school was not doing enough to make sure that the baseball team maintained its quality. I pointed out to her that the team had won the league championship for the past ten years. That information was irrelevant to her; her only concern was that her son have the experience of being on a league championship team.

Consumerism may turn what should be a cooperative relationship between parent and teacher into an adversarial one. The tendency to see the teacher as the adversary, as someone "out to get my child," is one of the most unfortunate aspects of current parental attitudes toward education. This viewpoint becomes most apparent when the teacher punishes a child. Many older educators have remarked that when they were growing up, the last thing in the world they wanted was for their parents to find out they had been punished at school. Their parents would have added another punishment at home. A more typical parent of today would rush into school to challenge the punishment, thus sending a clear message to the student about the parent's view of the fairness and wisdom of teachers. A very clear task for schools in the 1990s is to help parents approach teacher–parent relationships not as adversarial but as cooperative for the good of the child.

Sometimes parents can receive a considerable degree of sympathy and empathy from those who know their children. Each year we have a large Christmas service in the National Cathedral. Our students, most of the parents, and even a fair number of alumni attend. One year a four-year-old boy sitting in the front row decided to test the limits of his mother's patience. He stood up and mimicked the conductor while all the congregation was sitting down. He gave out a rousing version of "Jingle Bells" while everyone else was quietly singing "Silent Night." From where I sat with the other participants in the service, I could sense the growing embarrassment of his mother while the ripples of laughter rolled down the Cathedral at each new antic. Finally, while the Bishop was giving a blessing, the boy took to the main aisle and made a dash for the far door. His harried mother chased after him. The roar of laughter indicated that every mother in the congregation understood and appreciated what the headmaster's wife was going through as she went after our son.

There is another component of parenting at the end of the twentieth century that appears to be dramatically on the rise. One is never sure when parenting will be over. A number of years ago, the wife of a member of our Governing Board, whose youngest child had recently graduated from secondary school and entered college, urged me to speak to the parents of seniors about the "empty nest syndrome" and how difficult it can be to cope with. Five years later she stopped me on the street and said: "Forget the 'empty nest syndrome.' Warn the parents about the 'full nest syndrome.' Both my children have graduated from college and come back home to live with us."

The economic realities of the job market for college graduates, particularly in the liberal arts, interacting with the very expensive housing market have meant that increasing numbers of young adults are living with their parents. It can, of course, be a happy time of having a child back with the family after an absence of four years. But it can also be something of a strain on both parties. The parents still feel some sense of responsibility and expect a degree of conformity with the old rules of the household. The young adult has had four years of almost total freedom and a lifestyle usually built around very late hours. In somewhat similar fashion, the high divorce rate means that a number of older parents have suddenly had to resume parenting responsibilities when a newly divorced son or daughter needs help with child care or housing. If economic and divorce trends continue in their present directions, parents of the students of the 1990s need to be prepared for the possibility of those students returning home some time in the twenty-first century.

A Headmaster's Advice

There are numerous books that give advice on parenting. I suspect one could find a text to defend practically any parenting practice one chooses to adopt. I would like to offer a few suggestions from the point of view of an educator who spends a good deal of his time working with parents. As a parent myself, I recognize fully how difficult it is to put other people's advice into practice.

It is important to recognize that some tensions between parents and children are part of the natural human cycle of growth. They always have been and it appears they always will be. As John Silber, President of Boston University, has pointed out: "The generation gap was noticed early. It was high on the agenda at Mount Sinai; the practice of honoring fathers and mothers was so deficient as to call forth a commandment on the subject."[12] It is important for parents to know that there will be rough times in their relationships with their children. It is easier to cope with those times if one expects them, rather than sees them as a sign that something has suddenly gone terribly wrong.

I believe that it is very important for a parent always to keep in mind what his or her long-range goal is for the child. In a success-oriented society, we apply the measuring stick of short-run accomplishments and neglect what we truly want for our child. Is a particular grade or athletic victory or even college admission our goal, or is something else more important? I think it would be worthwhile for each parent to think about, write out, and occasionally revise his or her goals for the child. At the risk of oversimplification, I would like to suggest a one-sentence goal: that the child become an independent adult with the inner resources to create satisfactory personal relationships and achieve professional success and who has the moral fiber to contribute to the making of a better world.

Human life is finite, not infinite. It is important that young people learn that there are limits. All of us are limited by time. Most of us are limited in financial resources. One concern I have is that some parents appear to allow their children to grow up believing there are no financial limits. I know of high school students who are given credit cards and need make no accounting of what they charge. Successful personal and community relationships depend on the willingness of each of us to accept limits. Finally, there are limits to the extent any of us can control the world around us. Bad things do happen and all of us know unhappiness and failure. By setting limits for our children, we help prepare them for an adult world in which they will also face limits.

One of the ways limits are set is by saying "no" to children, even when that is painful for both parents and children. Craig Bowman writes in *Education Week:*

"When our children have drinking problems, we tell them to 'just say no.' Same with drugs. Now that the AIDS epidemic is supposed to be fought by educational means, everybody is preaching the Puritan Gospel: say 'no' to sex. Educators and parents, however, won't—or can't—say 'no' to kids. We don't see that by saying 'yes,' we actually deprive and even imprison kids. I'm talking about routine, day-to-day decisions that get made in schools and homes nation-wide. Small, even unnoticeable, though these actions may seem, each has the potential to put away a child. At one local school, lazy parents conspire with an equally indolent counselor to change a student's class schedule. It seems a math teacher, Mr. Frank, is too hard on Suzy Waffle. Mr. and Mrs. Waffle demand an appointment with the guidance counselor. He agrees that geometry is too demanding and changes the schedule. There it is. Did you see it? That microscopic, gutless act that told a child, quite plainly, 'you don't have to attend to the class called Reality. Between Daddy, Mommy, and a couple of educators, we can bail you out.' "[13]

Most people become teachers despite the low pay because they care about young people. Parents should keep this in mind when they meet with teachers. Clearly, parents and teachers will occasionally disagree, and there will be situations and conflicts that have to be worked out. But if either parent or teacher lets the situation change from one of cooperative partnership, with both sides seeking the best for the child, to an adversarial relationship, it will be to the detriment of the child. Just as parents sometimes have to do things to children that they do not like, so teachers will also have to act in a similar manner. And just as the relatives of someone who is ill are more likely to get good medical service when they work with the doctor rather than see him as the adversary, so parents will get better education for their children when they work with teachers for a mutually acceptable solution to problems.

One important way for parents to be involved with a school is through volunteer activities and parent meetings. These send a message to our children that not only are schools important, but that volunteerism is an obligation for responsible adults. Moreover, it allows parents an opportunity to get to know other parents, which is always helpful, and it brings parents in contact with teachers and administrators in a positive way. Finally, of course, volunteer activities improve the quality of the school and that is valuable for one's own children as well as others. One of the qualities that impresses me most about the parents I have known in the '80s and '90s is their willingness to give generously of their time and talents for the benefit of their children's schools. I am proud that a large majority of the families at St. Albans contribute both their time and their resources for the good of the school. Their helpfulness adds immeasurably to the quality of the education their children receive.

Even conscientious and loving parents may have children who get in trouble. It is a difficult time for a child but so is it for the parents. It causes them guilt and self-doubt about the way they have performed as parents. At such a time it is appropriate to give some thought to how one is parenting, but undue guilt or loss of courage may actually make the situation worse. The parent whose child is in trouble has the difficult role of supporting both the child and the school. It is important to let the child know that while you disapprove of the action, your love for your son or daughter is not conditional upon good behavior. It is equally important that you help your child learn that actions do have consequences. One can meet those consequences no matter how painful they are, and then go forward with a fresh start. I think it is particularly harmful to a child to have his or her parents nitpick the procedure or technicalities of the school's punishment rather than face the serious issues of what is going on in the child's life. It has been my frequent observation that if a school punishes a child, it will have little effect if the child gets the message from a parent that the punishment is wrong. All of us will have failures and setbacks in life, and when a child is in trouble, it is a wonderful time to teach him about both unconditional love and the way to respond in difficult situations.

I am seldom given to acronyms, but just for fun, let me try one: teach your child to COPE by giving your child *C*onsistency, *O*ffers of help, *P*raise, and *E*ncouragement. Young people do find the world to be confusing and unsteady, and consistency from parents gives them a sense of stability and security that they need. It is sometimes difficult to draw the line between consistency and rigidity. It seems to me the important thing is that consistency is clear in its goals and values, but can allow for some flexibility in reaching them. Some years ago, Midge Decter, in *Liberal Parents, Radical Children,* wrote an imaginary letter to children raised in the '60s. As those children now become parents, part of that letter is worth repeating:

"If you are self-regarding, this is because we refused to stand for ourselves, for both the propriety and hard-earned value of our own sense of life. Our contentions with you were based on appeal, not on authority. Believing you to be a new phenomenon among mankind—children raised exclusively on a principle of love, love unvaryingly acted out on our side and freely and voluntarily offered on yours—we enthroned you as such. We found our role more attractive this way, more suited to our self-image and enlightenment, and—though we would have died on the rack before confessing—far easier to play. In other words, we refused to assume, partly on ideological grounds but partly also, I think, on esthetic grounds, one of the central obligations of parenthood: to make ourselves the final authority on good and bad, right and wrong, and to take the consequences of what might turn out to be a lifelong battle. It might sound a paradoxical thing to say—for surely never has a generation of children occupied more sheer hours of parental time—but the truth is that we neglected you. We allowed you a charade of trivial freedoms in order to avoid making those impositions on you that are in the end both the training ground and proving ground for true independence. We pronounced you strong when you were still weak in order to avoid the struggles with you that would have fed your true strength. We proclaimed you sound when you were foolish in order to avoid taking part in the long, slow, slogging effort that is the only route to genuine maturity of mind and feeling. Thus, it was no small anomaly of your growing up that while you were the most indulged generation, you were also in many ways the most abandoned to your own meager devices by those into whose safekeeping you had been given. . . ."[14]

Offering to help lets a child know that the parent cares, but still gives the child the independence to choose or reject the help. That is an important step in the child's growth. All of us who are parents have had the experience of a child's coming home from school and reporting some incident that was very disturbing. Many of us had the reaction of saying "Well, I'll go into school and straighten that out," only to hear our child say: "Don't do that. I'll take care of it." If the child can take care of it, it will lead to growth. The offer to help need not just be with problems, but also with activities and goals the child is trying to accomplish. For a parent to offer rather than to insist on helping gives the child control of the situation and allows him to make an important decision about his own needs.

I believe that praise is the most powerful of human motivators. All of us need to feel valued and worthwhile. Most of us respond to praise by trying to earn more. I believe also that children have a very fine-tuned sense of what is false praise, and that is not helpful. I am aware that most of us who are parents or teachers give more criticism than we do praise, and I do not believe that is in the best interest of children.

Encouragement can help young people overcome their natural self-doubts. What a positive reinforcer it is to have someone say: "I believe you can do that; I have faith in you." We all know that we can accomplish things only when we have faith in ourselves. Children are naturally insecure as they learn about their own abilities and an infusion of faith from someone else may make all the difference.

Finally, my advice as both headmaster and parent is that humor and patience are among the most important qualities a parent can have. Do remember that some day you will have the pleasure of watching your children raise their children, with all the dilemmas, uncertainties, and frustrations that you have had.

Chapter Four

A Confusing and Unsteady World

To try to predict the future is stargazing, yet to educate young people with no vision of what the world will be like when they are adults is to travel in the darkness. Inevitably when we make predictions, we make them on the basis of trends we observe now and believe will continue. If they do not develop, or if new, more powerful trends emerge, our predictions will be inaccurate. Frankly, that is not a prospect that worries me. The purpose of this chapter is not to give an accurate picture of life in the year 2010; rather, it is to stimulate teachers and parents to think about the world their children will inherit. The best way to do this is to offer one's own vision of the forces that will be at work as today's students become adults.

The first development is already here, but it will grow in force as we enter the twenty-first century. In 1956, for the first time in our history, white-collar workers outnumbered blue-collar. That could be said to be the start of the information age, as more Americans earned their living with information rather than by making things. By the 1980s, more people were employed by universities than worked in agriculture. What an amazing statement about the importance of information and learning, as well as about the efficiency of American agriculture: that higher education, not to mention the even larger field of elementary and secondary education, demands more workers than feeding the nation.

The importance of this fact is not just that so many people are involved in the collection, processing, and dissemination of information. It is that the amount of information is growing at such a rapid rate. For example, the field of immunology is changing so fast that journals are often out of date before they are published.

What skills will be necessary to function in the information age of the twenty-first century? Certainly, educated people will need to be able to use the technology that handles vast amounts of information rapidly. That technology is itself changing at an astronomical rate. Equally important will be the ability to sort through vast amounts of material very quickly and extrapolate what is important or useful. Finally, the ability and willingness to continue learning throughout life will be a key ingredient to success for those who are students in the 1990s.

Another change to which today's students must accommodate has also already come to pass, and will intensify as we move into the twenty-first century. This is the shift from people's dependence on each other locally or nationally to a truly global interdependence. The author of *Megatrends,*[1] John Naisbitt, gives us a fine example. What could be more American than a baseball glove? Yet how does a glove reach the hand of an American youngster? Ninety-five percent of all baseball gloves used in this country are made of American leather which is sent to Brazil for curing and then on to Taiwan or Korea for manufacturing into a glove. That the all-American game of baseball cannot be played without the contributions of people in Brazil, Taiwan, and Korea and that people in those countries depend on American baseball for their livelihood are both symbolic and actual ways in which our world has become interdependent.

This interdependence inevitably changes the way we think about the world and ourselves. In the spring of 1988, I stopped to talk with an Irish fisherman at a pier on Galway Bay. Soon he had invited me to his cottage for a glass of poteen, the homemade Irish liquor. Nothing could more match the romantic notion of traditional Ireland than having a glass of poteen with a fisherman as the sun sank in Galway Bay. But the fisherman's talk was modern. He told of how joining the Common Market had meant that it was easier to sell his catch in France, but that it allowed continental fishing boats, which are often better equipped, to enter Irish waters. He summed it up by saying, "We're not Irish anymore, we're Europeans."

When I went to Japan in 1988 to set up an exchange with the Keio School, I was guided by a young American who had been my student just six years earlier. Now he was living in Japan, making frequent trips to China as a salesman for a Japanese company. The legacy of World War II was such that in China, an American was a more welcome representative from a Japanese company than a Japanese native. A young American who can sell Japanese products in China is just the sort of cosmopolitan businessman our country needs to produce.

Those who will be successful economically in the twenty-first century will be those who learn to think of themselves as economic citizens of the world and who develop the skills and understanding necessary for business dealings with people from all over the world. Moreover, increasing numbers of Americans will find themselves working for companies that are owned by non-Americans. Even in the 1980s there were congressional districts in America where the largest employer was Japanese. It has been estimated that by the start of the twenty-first century, the Japanese will own one-tenth of the resources of America and significant amounts of the remaining resources will be in the control of other non-Americans. Thus, American workers and executives must be able not only to trade with other countries, but also to work for and with non-Americans within the United States.

Of course, the shrinking of the world is evident not only in economic matters. The space age has provided telecommunications satellites that make virtually instantaneous transmittal of information and visual images possible to any place on the globe. Thus, events anywhere in the world take on an immediacy for all other places. Sometimes this produces a shared experience that helps bind people together, as when millions of people all over the world share the experience of the Olympics or a royal wedding. But it also means that anyone can get his message heard around the world. A terrorist hijacker can get his face and words into the homes and minds of people literally halfway around the world.

It is not just products for trade and information that move rapidly all over the world. People do too. This may increase understanding and communication, but it also means that the problems of one area are rapidly transmitted to another area. It is harder to ignore conflict in the Middle East or changes in Eastern Europe when one knows citizens of those countries who are now students in the United States. Of course, the most dramatic and dangerous example of the spreading of world problems in the 1980s was the speed at which AIDS became a worldwide disease.

Diversity in America

Not only will Americans in the twenty-first century have to interact successfully with a very diverse world, but America itself is becoming more diverse. The melting pot is no longer turning out a typical American. With the exception of a few groups such as the Pennsylvania Dutch or ultraconservative Jews, most immigrants saw, and wanted, their children to move into the mainstream of American life. Public education was the great common experience. For children to be taught in English and to be exposed to American legends and myths provided a common cultural background that accomplished the homogenization of diverse peoples. There might have been differences in style between the Irish Catholic in Boston, the Jew in Scarsdale, the Norwegian Lutheran in Minneapolis, the black in Washington's Gold Coast, and the oriental in California, but all shared a common language, a common American dream, and a common vision of what America meant. And despite the differences in style, the vision was remarkably WASPish: strong education leading to personal success, gentlemanly behavior which was polite but kept emotions in control, and an overlay of culture and religion without either being carried to extremes.

Perhaps by coincidence both internal and external forces began simultaneously to challenge the notion of a melting pot and both have had effects on education. One aspect of the civil rights movement was the demand for black pride and black studies. It was clear that the contribution of blacks to American life had not been recognized in the education given to our children, whether white or black. As is often the case, the important attempts to correct the situation produced some extremes. By the 1980s black leaders saw that the creation of a major in black studies rather than a more marketable discipline or the argument that standard English should not be imposed on ghetto youngsters actually reduced the opportunities that blacks had for advancement in American society. It is important for both black and white educators in the 1990s to work out the best way to help all youngsters recognize the contributions that diverse groups have made to American culture while still introducing students to the body of material needed for cultural literacy in America.

There has also been a separatist movement within white America. While the established churches and the society in general became more liberal, this country has seen an enormous increase in fundamentalism. The varieties of fundamentalist expression make it difficult to generalize the movement, but several aspects should be mentioned. First, it is the only type of Christianity that is growing in the United States. Both the Roman Catholic and the mainline Protestant churches are facing declining numbers. Second, it is the only type of religion that has made effective use of that most powerful media, television. Even the televangelistic scandals of the 1980s appear to have had little long-range consequence. Third, although not necessarily anti-intellectual, fundamentalism puts a much greater emphasis on the emotional rather than the rational. It also stresses the literal acceptance of Scripture rather than analytical interpretation. This particularly affects schools because of their presumed emphasis on rationality. Fourth, many of its members are ready to opt out of the mainstream of American life if their values are threatened too strongly. What began as segregationist academies have now become schools where fundamentalist beliefs and disciplines can be taught. Ironically, most of the people who make separatism a part of their lives would argue that they were defending the American way. Fifth, fundamentalism usually stresses a conservative personal morality. Social concerns are not totally ignored, but clearly the emphasis is on a traditional value structure and code of conduct for the individual. It is too soon to know if fundamentalism has reached its peak in America or whether it will continue to grow, but clearly it will be a force in American life in the twenty-first century.

There is also a rapid growth in the number of Moslems in America. By the time the secondary students of the 1990s reach age forty, it is quite likely that there will be more Moslems than Jews in America.[2] It is difficult to predict what effect it would have on American life to have a significant minority of our citizens whose heritage goes back to the Koran rather than to the Bible.

All four of these changes in American society challenge the notion of a shared culture to which every American should be assimilated. It is important to note that that culture was traditionally of European derivation. English was used as its language, and when foreign languages were taught, they were most often European. Moreover, the virtues traditionally associated with the best of England were generally valued. That culture will not have a monolithic hold on American life in the twenty-first century. By the time today's students are reaching retirement age, non-Hispanic whites will be less than 50 percent of the American population. Just as the students of the 1990s must be educated to interact with the diverse cultures of the world, they must also be prepared for a very different cultural life in America.

The Individual

As this century draws to a close, our view of the world presents a challenging paradox. As the world appears to shrink in terms of economics or communication, the world with which the individual must interact appears to expand. Marshall McLuhan may be right that television has created a "global village." But for the individual, the number of people who can affect his life has increased so astronomically that it would be more accurate to say there is a global megalopolis. The man whose grandfather worked in a ten-man shop and whose father worked for a manufacturing firm with a thousand employees now works for a multinational corporation with tens of thousands of employees spread across the globe. This can lead to a sense of impotence for the individual because as an individual he has so little ability to influence those who will make the political or economic decisions that will most affect him. Although it is not yet on a global scale, the same feeling of powerlessness confronts people as they consider the education of their children. The man whose grandfather may have known personally every member of the village school board now lives in a populous state in which a central board, located several hundred miles from his home, decides which textbooks will be used in all the high schools within that state.

As the world becomes more interconnected, the feeling of individual impotence will grow even more profound in the 1990s and beyond. People will respond to this feeling in one or both of two ways. At times they will seek smaller associations of special interest, such as ethnic, hobby, self-help, political action, or religious groups, which will allow members to be involved in the decision-making process and give them a sense of specialness and meaning to their lives. Such groups will become even more important as individuals develop a sense of belonging and control. People will also seek ways to have some influence on those large organizations that often control their lives. Whether the organization is governmental, economic, or educational, many people will continue to seek reforms that move away from oligarchy or representational democracy and toward participatory democracy. In politics this trend has moved the national parties toward more primaries and caucuses as a way to choose a candidate. It has also caused a significant increase in the use of the initiative and referendum as ways for voters to express their views on particular issues. In business we see increased organized consumerism, greater shareholder action, and most conspicuously, greater worker participation and vastly expanded employee rights. In education parents are becoming more individually involved and also asking for more powerful parent associations so that group pressure can be applied. The idea that one simply entrusts one's child to a school to be educated by those who know best is no longer acceptable to most parents.

Choices

One of the hopes parents frequently express about their children's education is their wish that schools would do more to inculcate values. Part of this reflects their realization that they are not doing the job as effectively as they would like. In Chapter Six we will look at some of the reasons why this is so, but it is also true that even the most conscientious parents can only do so much to shape their children. Certainly adolescents spend more hours in school and in peer activities than they do with their parents. Thus, parents look to the schools to do the job of value formation they feel they are unable to accomplish. This concern is even more justified when one remembers that the interconnectedness of all people in the world continues to increase. In a shrinking world, consequences of our actions take on even greater significance. Nuclear weapons, communicable diseases, and environmental pollution provide the most obvious examples of this phenomenon, but it is also true that such ethical matters as compassion for others and honesty in communication take on new importance in an interconnected world. While the issue of ethics requires its own chapter, there is one point related to ethics that I wish to discuss at this time because it is important for the children of the 1990s.

In his book *Megatrends,* John Naisbitt refers to the multi-option society. On the most obvious level we now have a tremendous number of options in the goods we purchase. As Naisbitt half jokingly points out, it used to be that bathtubs were white, telephones black, and checks green.[3] Now one has to make several choices to acquire any of these objects: "What color would you like? Do you want a matching or coordinate checkbook? Do you want pine trees, wild flowers, or a herd of deer printed on the check?"

The multi-option nature of our lives extends far beyond consumer goods and touches the most important aspects of our existence. A century and a half ago most men knew that they would earn a living in the occupation their father had pursued. Almost all women could look forward only to a life as a housewife and mother. Half a century ago men knew they had a variety of options when they chose an occupation. However, once the choice was made, it was relatively permanent and for many, once they joined a particular firm, they were unlikely to leave it. A few occupations such as school teaching or nursing were open to women, but even these were often seen as temporary before going on to the life work of being a housewife and mother. Today, of course, changing employers is relatively common, and an increasing number of people change their occupations at mid-life. I have heard many of my contemporaries say, just as they reached a certain level of success in their careers, such as becoming partners in a law firm, tenured professors, established in a medical practice, even headmasters: "I've worked hard to get here and I like it. But I can't imagine doing this for the next thirty years." The range of options open to women has increased most dramatically. Most professions are relatively open to them and they now have important choices to make about timing: for example, career for a while, motherhood for a while, then back to career, or do I do both at the same time? Or is part-time at each best?

If this range of choices is true in professional life, it is equally true in family matters. A whole range of lifestyle options are now acceptable. Moreover, if one particular lifestyle is chosen and then it no longer pleases, it can be changed. At the present time, only 7 percent of Americans live in the traditional model of the father employed outside the home, the mother not having a paying job, and the children in the family being descended from both parents.[4] Similarly, the number of Americans who live alone has risen from 10 percent in the 1950s to 25 percent at the present time.[5] The fact that family life is now multi-optional has very significant implications for schools in their interactions with parents and students, and also, in the expectations that are put on schools. The fact that all areas of our society are multi-optional and will probably become more so in the twenty-first century adds another dimension to questions about teaching and the role of schools.

On the one hand, young adults will have to face a world full of choices and change. Should schools help students to become better decision-makers? Graduate schools of business, law, and now public administration train people in decision-making within specific professional areas. Are there ways that schools can train students to make better choices in their personal lives in the areas of family, career, and lifestyle? In the late 1960s some schools gave young people many more decisions to make while they were students. Greater choices in both academic matters and use of free time were offered. It was not an experiment with notable success. Some schools try to provide training in decision-making somewhat similar to that of graduate schools and use the case method of discussion. There is little evidence one way or another about the effectiveness of this at the secondary level. The opportunity for choice must be balanced against the recognition that all human beings need some consistency in their lives. When family life is in flux and young adults are quite likely to change living arrangements, geographical location, and careers several times before they are forty, the school experience may be the most stable thing in a person's life until he or she is well into middle age. So the challenge for the school is to provide both preparation for a world of choice and change, and the stability, sense of permanence, and appreciation of tradition that they may find nowhere else in life.

Loyalty

There is one other aspect to the multiple-option nature of our society that must be addressed. Whether or not schools can make a difference is unclear, but they should certainly understand the issue as they prepare students for the twenty-first century. While we all enjoy having a range of options whenever we have a choice to make, there is increasing evidence that the decline in the sense of loyalty that such a situation creates is not in the best interest of the society. It may well be that the twenty-first century will belong to those societies that offer their members fewer choices.

America's relative decline in global economic power may be partially attributable to improvement in other countries and the reality that our natural resources are not unlimited. But there is another factor that has to do with choice. Those countries that have risen most spectacularly economically recently are those where long-term loyalty to a particular company is stressed. One joins a firm as a young adult and expects to spend all of one's working life there. The worker or executive is loyal to that firm, and he or she has reason to expect that the company will return that loyalty. Thus, the employee knows that his or her long-term prosperity is tied to the success of the firm, and the executive knows that long-range planning and considering what is best for the future growth of the company is what is best for him. There is incentive for capital improvement, reinvestment of profits, and decisions based on long-range factors.

By contrast, the executive in America is often judged by quarterly or, if he or she is lucky, annual profit statements. It is a dictum of American business that having the same chief executive for too long will lead to stagnation. Even "pop" business advice such as Robert Townsend's *Further Up the Organization* teaches this dictum: "If the CEO does not retire gracefully after five or seven years, throw the rascal out."[6] Executives, and perhaps even teachers, know that they will probably maximize their earnings by changing employers several times in their careers. They also know that a company may at any time fall victim to a corporate raider or a merger, and that even executives whose performances have been strong may be out of work. Thus, there is incentive for short-range decisions that make the executive look good at any given moment.

Perhaps an example from the school world would illustrate what I am saying about business. Every headmaster of an independent school wants to operate in the black, keep faculty salaries up and tuition low. These things make him look good to trustees. If a headmaster increases the amount of funds from the annual budget to be placed in replacement reserve for future maintenance problems, he makes it more difficult to meet the three goals I just mentioned. It is, however, in the long-range best interest of the school to take steps today to ensure that future bills can be paid. The headmaster who expects to have a short term in office will find it against his self-interest to do so. The one who expects to have a long tenure, or who puts the interest of the school above self-interest, will care about the long-range needs of the school.

In similar fashion, freedom of choice about family matters and lifestyle may increase the happiness of many individuals, but may be harmful to society. The evidence is clear that those ethnic groups within our society that have the most stable family situation have the most successful and accomplished children. Of course, there are many individual exceptions. We all know of examples of individuals from unstable families who have been successful and, unfortunately, individuals who demonstrate the reverse. Nonetheless, stability and a sense of family loyalty are clearly good for children. By loyalty, I mean the sense that family will always stand by the youngster and that the child has responsibilities not only to himself but to his family to make a success of his life. These, however, are difficult to achieve while also expecting everyone to have a wide range of options about how they live their lives.

I have mentioned several developments that may be significant factors in the twenty-first century. Any thoughtful reader can, and should, add others. It is also true that many of the problems we have faced in the last half of the twentieth century will continue to be serious threats in the years ahead, such as nuclear arms, deterioration of the environment, regional wars, poverty, AIDS, terrorism, alcoholism, and substance abuse. While I do not believe that secondary schools should build curricula around perceived problems or threats, it is important that educators and parents keep always in mind that they are not preparing students for the present but for the future, and the more thoughtful we are about the future, the better we can prepare our students for the world they will inherit.

Chapter Five

Sound Learning

The 1960s saw a great opening up and expansion of the curricular offerings of American colleges and secondary schools. Not only was there a wider range of courses offered, but students were also given a much greater choice in shaping their own course of study. Specific requirements for graduation were reduced as students demanded a much greater control over which subjects they studied. At the same time, there was a movement away from the accumulation of information and greater emphasis on development of thinking and question-asking skills.

Inevitably, the late 1970s brought a reaction. Harvard received much attention for its new Core Curriculum, and other institutions sought ways to reintroduce the idea that there is a body of material, or at least a number of academic disciplines, with which educated men and women should be familiar. During the 1980s the debate continued. The appeal of Allan Bloom's *The Closing of the American Mind*[1] and E. D. Hirsch's *Cultural Literacy*[2] showed that many Americans worried that we had gone too far in letting students define their own education. Moreover, it appeared that these students were appallingly lacking in basic knowledge. In 1987, U.S. Secretary of Education William Bennett proposed a model curriculum for secondary schools that prescribed what he believed were the essential elements of precollegiate education.[3] It required four years of English, three years of mathematics, three years of science, three years of social studies (broken down into Western civilization, American history, and American democracy), two years of a foreign language, two years of physical education and health, and one year of fine arts. The rest of the schedule was to be made up of electives. This is hardly a revolution in education. What is noteworthy is that the Secretary of Education felt it necessary to indicate these as a *minimum* for secondary education. Apparently, many high schools fall far short of these standards. It is distressing that he did not include any computer education in his requirements.[4] Clearly, those going on to a university need to have some computer literacy. I would argue that it is equally necessary for those not going to university. Skill on a word processor is a very marketable commodity; one visit to a modern automated factory makes it clear that even blue-collar workers need experience with computers.

It is not my purpose in this chapter to lay out a model curriculum for college-bound secondary students, but to make some comments about teaching in various disciplines. Beforehand, I would like to mention some of the factors that caused the open curriculum to have considerable appeal to both educators and students.

The Open Curriculum

All of us are aware of the dramatic increase in the amount of sheer information there is. A middle-aged English teacher could keep his students busy throughout their high school years just reading the best fiction that has been written since the teacher graduated from college. The expansion of knowledge in the sciences has been even more rapid. With the amount of knowledge so great and increasing so rapidly, no particular fixed curriculum can possibly embrace even a reasonable part of human knowledge. Those who favor an open curriculum argue that talk of a body of knowledge known by all educated persons is an impossibility today, and therefore, it becomes foolish for any curriculum to presume to give students that core of information.

It is here that I find Hirsch most persuasive. Some knowledge of certain historical facts, great works of literature and art, and scientific terms and principles is necessary for understanding and communication in our culture. A person who has never read any Shakespeare, knows nothing of the fundamental causes of the Civil War, or has no understanding of basic genetics is not an educated person in American culture. That person cannot understand or appreciate our cultural life, how we reached our present position as a nation, or the evolutionary development of living organisms. Moreover, that person will have wide gaps in his ability to communicate with or understand those who are educated, because the educated take such knowledge for granted. Yet a curriculum in which most courses are electives would make it possible for a student to miss all of these areas. While the expansion of knowledge makes the development of a sound curriculum more difficult than it was in the past, it is still possible to decide that all one's students should have exposure to certain information and certain disciplines. Not every academic institution will decide on the same areas as essential for its curriculum. Some disagreement makes for the rich diversity that has so strengthened American life, but part of the identity of any academic institution must be a vision of what it considers an educated person to be.

Another argument is that a more traditional curriculum

demonstrates a strong bias toward cultural egocentricity in a world that is rapidly shrinking. Knowledge of other cultures and the historical development of other nations is essential. Most prescribed curricula will place an emphasis on the culture and history of one's own country and thus not give students the breadth of knowledge they need to be adults in the twenty-first century.

It is indeed true that most curricula in this country are weighted toward the American experience, but this is as it should be. Students best understand and appreciate other cultures if they are familiar with their own. Without a grounding in one's own culture, information about others becomes a disorganized collage because there are no points of reference with which to assess or understand it. Even more important is the fact that an open curriculum does little to guarantee that most students will have a broad exposure. Rather, most will follow their own interests, and this means pursuing something that has already caught their fancy. Those who do venture into new areas are likely to do so in a random way. While any prescribed curriculum will have its own cultural and national bias, it is more likely to demand that students be exposed to ideas and values that are unfamiliar to them and that this exposure be in an organized manner that helps a student make sense of the whole.

A third argument goes to the heart of the question about learning. It states that method is more important than content because the development of critical and analytical methods of thinking gives a student the skills that are necessary to solve new problems or face new situations. Thus, for example, the goal of teaching history is not to give the student names and dates and causes. It is to equip the student with the ability to digest the raw data of history and draw insightful conclusions from those data. This ability can be developed with material from any historical period. Thus, there is no need to prescribe history courses that cover any particular periods. Any history course can serve the same goal.

While this argument holds true if one's goal is only method, it is clearly inappropriate if one is interested in either cultural literacy or an understanding of the growth of the particular society. A curriculum that allows students an option to choose between courses on ancient Egypt and courses on colonial America may teach historical methods, but it will not ensure that students develop an understanding of why their own society took the shape that it did.

In any academic discipline, to make the issue of method versus content an "either/or" situation is to oversimplify. It is possible and desirable to teach courses that present students with information they need for cultural literacy and still encourage the critical thinking and methodology appropriate to that discipline.

I once had the fun of teaching a summer school course on revolutions. I tried to look at both the methodology by which one might study a revolution, and the facts of some particular revolutions. The first day of class I asked the students to brainstorm about how they would start a revolution. After some discussion, one young man who seemed a little cagier than the rest said: "You've got to get the government to kill a child. A revolution needs a martyr."

After class, I caught the boy alone in the hall and said: "I want to make a deal with you. If you can create a revolution in this class, I'll give you an A. Four weeks from today, I'm going to give a major test. Your assignment is to make sure that none of the class takes the test. You can do anything you want except tell anyone that I put you up to this."

With some pangs of conscience, I decided not to tell the college student who was helping me with the course that summer as a teaching intern. The revolutionary, whose name was Steve, tried persuasion with little effect. Then he tried bribery. However, if he offered enough money to make it worthwhile to another student, he would never have the funds to ever pay that amount. Finally, like a good revolutionary, Steve tried deception. He told Bill that Fred had agreed to join the revolution if Bill would, and then went to Fred with the reverse message. I thought I ought to give Steve a helping hand. I had promised the class a thorough review session the day before the test, but instead I deliberately wasted the class period. That gave Steve the chance he needed, and he set to work that evening and soon had most of the class recruited.

I asked the teaching intern if he would administer the test and deliberately arrived a few minutes late. The intern passed out the tests and Steve went behind him, collecting them. He sat at his desk, holding a stack of tests. The intern stood in front of the class, trying—as authority figures often do—to reason the matter out. He was pleading, "Let's talk this over."

I thought it time to demonstrate the forces of establishment tyranny. I took the one remaining copy held by the intern and said to the class: "I am going down to make twenty more copies. You've got that time to decide whether you're going to take this test or flunk the course." As I went out of the room, I slammed the door behind me. I returned in a few minutes, and said in my gruffest voice, "Now who wants to take this test?"

One girl stifled a tear and said: "I've got to have the credit. I want to take it." With that, the united front of the revolutionaries was broken and all the students except Steve took another copy of the test and began to work.

I said to Steve, again in an angry voice, "Come out in the hall with me." We just managed to get the door shut before we began to laugh. I told him to tell his classmates that I was going to have him expelled. At lunch immediately after the class, the teaching intern came up to me and said: "Now we really have a problem. Everyone is furious that you are going to expel Steve. They really are ready to revolt."

I pointed out, "Now the revolution has a martyr."

"But what are we going to do?" asked the intern.

I smiled and said: "I don't know what you're going to do, but in the next class meeting I'm going to explain to everyone how Steve and I planned the whole thing." The poor intern almost dropped his tray of food in surprise, but did accept my duplicity in good grace. In the next class meeting, we had a most interesting discussion, led by Steve, about what had worked and what had not in the process of revolution. It was fun for the students to apply those lessons to the American, French, Russian, and German revolutions they were studying.

Of course, dramatic teaching can sometimes backfire. I remember a young teacher who suddenly collapsed onto the floor during an English class. A student took one look at him and dashed for the school nurse. The nurse, hearing of the emergency, ran across the school courtyard, up two flights of stairs, and arrived close to collapse herself. She found the young teacher calmly teaching the class, and explaining how he had faked the incident to demonstrate a point. The boy had been totally taken in and had responded appropriately. It did take that teacher some months to restore his relationship with the nurse.

However, he did not curtail his enthusiasm for the unusual. When assigned to teach public speaking, he thought it important that his students face a tough audience. He would have his whole class board a city bus as it worked its way down Wisconsin Avenue toward Georgetown. After getting permission from the bus driver (and that was never denied) a high school student would have to give a public address standing at the front of the bus. The riders would be asked to vote with applause on the quality of the speech. Whether or not our boys improved their speaking ability, there is no question that the school provided entertainment for Washington commuters.

Another issue that arises in the debate about open curriculum is the choice between "survey" courses and "in-depth" courses. This is a more difficult issue at the secondary level than it is in undergraduate education. Survey courses are accused of covering too much material too fast so that the student leaves the course with little more than an overview and a handful of facts. It is true that in a survey course it is more difficult to develop the skill of critical thinking, yet it is also obvious that survey courses are more appropriate for most secondary school students, for they must overcome considerable cultural illiteracy. Students are at the age when they need to learn the basic vocabulary and definitions of each discipline so that they can understand what others are saying when they discuss the subject. Moreover, survey courses are more likely to expose students to new material and ideas that have not been presented to them before. This is important before they are offered the range of electives that are available in college. The broad experience of a survey course will allow a student to make more thoughtful choices among electives.

There are also a number of reasons for the popularity of the open curriculum that are not directly related to one's view of knowledge. As argued in Chapter Four, a multitude of choices are now a permanent part of modern life. Many people believe that the best way to learn to make choices is, indeed, to make them. Thus, by being allowed choices about what they will study, students are being prepared for a lifetime of decision-making. I would argue, however, that information is necessary if one is to make good choices. The secondary school curriculum should provide students with that information, and with the skills to acquire more information. While a good secondary school should be very concerned about preparing students for a world in which they will make choices, the curriculum must be designed to give them the material necessary to make informed decisions. The very fact that making choices is difficult is another reason why academic institutions find a more open curriculum easier to administer. To formulate a curriculum is to make judgments about the relative importance of different disciplines and areas of study. It is to declare that some subject matter is essential while other material is merely useful, but not necessary. Those who make such judgments lay themselves open to various charges, ranging from cultural bias to personal bias to narrow-mindedness. Because any of these accusations will carry with it some degree of truth, and because they are hard to refute, educators like to avoid being put in the position where they have to take a stand for some academic areas and against others. However, to say that all knowledge is equally necessary is a position that few educators would espouse. To refuse to articulate one's choice is cowardice.

There is another reason why teachers find an open curriculum appealing. To put it bluntly, teaching electives is more satisfying than teaching required courses. Electives attract students who want to take the course and thus it is a greater pleasure to teach them. Electives allow teachers to work on their special interests and that is fulfilling. Electives mean that teachers can present new material and thus keep intellectually alive. However, the important thing to remember, of course, is that a curriculum should be designed to maximize the education of students rather than the satisfaction of teachers.

One other motive that leads secondary schools to offer

more electives is that electives help schools ensure that students with a significant range of abilities are all able to graduate. By offering highly demanding courses for the very able, but not requiring weaker students to take them, schools find material that is "suitable" for each student.

We have seen that there are incentives for a secondary school to offer more and more electives. I believe that there are two major reasons why this is unwise. The first and most important is that precollegiate education is the time for laying the foundations necessary for later work. This is the time when students must acquire both the information and the academic skills they will need to be able to pursue postsecondary work in a particular academic area while still having some understanding of other areas. Universities should cover the universe of knowledge. Secondary schools must provide what is essential to be an educated adult. It is the job of such schools to define what information and skills are essential and then to insist that their students receive them.

The second reason for a core curriculum has to do with the shared experience that secondary education should provide. The interaction of students, just as they are beginning to be intellectually alive, is invaluable. It is not possible to have this exchange of ideas if each student is free to choose whatever he or she wishes to study.

The analogy I like best is of a meal. A large cafeteria will have a vast number of selections. Each person takes or rejects whatever he or she wishes and then sits with whomever he or she desires. In a family meal, everyone shares the same fare (with a few minor exceptions, as in "no lima beans, please"). Everyone sits at the same table whether they particularly like each other or not. The large cafeteria will have an impressive range of tempting foods, but to learn to communicate and interact with others, the common table is far superior. The shared meal or a limited curriculum leads to intellectual growth because of the mental interaction it encourages. It is an interesting parallel that the most important identifiable common factor among National Merit finalists, other than parents' education, is that the family regularly shared meals together. Interaction between adults and children provided important stimulation.

Elements of a Secondary School Curriculum

I want to suggest nine elements that I believe should make up the curriculum of the children of the moon—those who are students in the 1990s and will be adults in the twenty-first century.

Verbal Communication

This first element is the most important, for without skill in verbal communication all other knowledge will be difficult to acquire and even more difficult to use effectively. Think for a moment of a research scientist. While training in the scientific method is crucial, the scientist must also be able to read and understand the work of other scientists, write up his own findings so that others can understand them, write grant proposals to obtain funds for research, and finally discuss ideas and convince colleagues and committees.

Verbal communication includes the ability to read for understanding. Not only comprehension, but discernment is important. The student must learn the skill of working through material and deciding what is important for the purposes at hand. For example, the history teacher who gives his students a list of names to learn is not being as helpful as the one who insists that students develop the

Elements of a Secondary School Curriculum

Verbal Communication
Computation
Our Own Culture
Computer Literacy
Science
Our Small World
The Arts
Decision-Making
Visual Communication

ability to decide for themselves which names are worth remembering and which can be forgotten. In the information age, students will be presented with vast amounts of material throughout their lives. The ability to discern what is essential and what is unnecessary will be one of the most important skills they must have.

Being able to read well also includes the skill of being able to follow another's organization, to understand if conclusions really follow from premises, to distinguish a generalization from a description and to bring other information to bear on the material being read. Teachers must be sure that their students not only read, but also read thoughtfully. The classic phrase is "read, mark, learn and inwardly digest."

Just as important as reading well is the ability to write effectively. Of course, accurate grammar and syntax are necessary. But having a good sense of style, conveying ideas and setting forth convincing arguments must also be stressed. Those who correct student writing have a remarkable opportunity to teach clarity of expression, precision of presentation, and logical thinking. To miss that opportunity is to betray one's students. While good teaching is important if students are to learn to write, I believe that writing is definitely an activity that improves with practice. A good secondary school curriculum will insist that students write frequently, in English and other classes. As students mature, longer assignments help them learn to organize and present their thoughts.

Finally, attention should be given to oral communication. Small classes which encourage discussion are terribly important. Teachers must also be aware of those students who are not participating, and work to get them more involved. Public speaking classes are also very useful and I would argue that any English course should include some public speaking, even if it is only by asking each student to read a paper aloud in class from time to time. Since almost all inexperienced people have a dread of speaking or reading in front of others, any experience that a school can give a student in these areas will be very important in helping him overcome his fear of having others hear his voice. Without the ability to communicate, in writing and in speaking, all else that a student does will be hampered.

Computation

The second most important curricular area for a secondary school is computation. In an increasingly scientific and technological world, skill in mathematics becomes ever more essential. A publication from Yale University points out:

"Mathematics is the basic language of the natural and social sciences, and has become a useful tool in many of the humanities. So pervasive are mathematical techniques that contemporary men and women may not consider themselves truly educated until they have an understanding of the fundamentals of mathematics. At a minimum, students should have a proficiency in mathematics at the level of calculus. . . . Whatever course a student chooses in order to broaden his mathematical knowledge, however, skill in mathematics should be maintained because, like skill in language, it is likely to dissipate if not used."[5]

The tragedy is the low level of math proficiency in the United States. Less than half of all high school students in America study geometry or algebra II. In West Germany or Japan 100 percent of high school students take these subjects. As the Second International Mathematics Study concluded: "The mathematical yield of U.S. schools may be rated among the lowest of any advanced industrial country."[6]

One of the major challenges to secondary schools is helping students and parents understand that mathematics is essential for the modern world and that hard work is essential for success in mathematics. A study was conducted about popular attitudes toward mathematics in both the United States and Japan. In the United States, the vast majority of those polled said that the most important ingredient for success in mathematics was ability. In Japan, the vast majority said it was *ganbaru,* which translates roughly as "to persevere."

This leads to another reason for studying mathematics. As Donald J. Brown, Chairman of the Mathematics Department at St. Albans School, has pointed out:

"Not only is mathematics important because it is the language within which the discourse of all modern science and much of the analytic discourse of modern social science takes place, there is an equally important reason.

Mathematics is the method *par excellence* of imparting to the human mind the habit of precise, logical, analytical reasoning. To put it another way: we teach our students mathematics both as an end and as a means to an end; but it is primarily for its ability to develop sustained mental discipline and intellectual rigor that mathematics possesses an importance transcending its own intrinsic merits. Although the demands of mathematics are strenuous, and its satisfactions not always immediate, the intellectual growth, which is its end result, is greater by far than the inevitable intellectual struggles along the way."[7]

Our Own Culture

A third essential in any secondary school curriculum is a grounding in one's own culture. To understand who we are as individuals and who we are as a people, it is necessary to know where we came from, why we developed as we did, and what we thought and said as we developed. It is not cultural egocentricity, but the path to self-knowledge, that makes European and American history and literature essential to a curriculum. Of course, this should include the experience of all ethnic groups in this country. As an aside, I want to point out one of the greatest paradoxes of public education in the United States. One would be hard-pressed to name a book that has had a bigger influence on our history and culture than the Bible, yet for very good reasons, knowledge of the Bible is not imparted in public secondary schools. As fewer and fewer young people are raised as active church members, except among the fundamentalists, we are educating a generation most of whom will have no exposure to one of the most important influences in Western development.

Computer Literacy

The fourth element of a curriculum is one Secretary of Education Bennett omitted. Computer literacy is an important job skill for those who do not go on to university, and it is an essential skill for those preparing for higher education. Already, a number of colleges are totally computer wired. This means that a student may sit at a terminal in his dormitory room, scan what used to be the card catalog in the library, order the books he wants to be waiting when he arrives at the library, type his paper at his terminal, and have it printed in his professor's office. The professor can then make his comments and award a grade, which will be retrieved on the screen in the student's dormitory room. While not every college is yet equipped with this sort of computer capability, it is clear that any educated person in the twenty-first century must have overcome computer anxiety and achieved computer literacy. The content of the phrase "computer literacy" will change as technology develops, but even a changing goal can be pursued.

Science

It is clear that science will continue to be of fundamental importance during the twenty-first century. After the Soviet Union put Sputnik into space, there was an attempt to revitalize science education in the United States. Dangerously, that effort faded in the 1980s. William Bennett wrote: "American students do not know very much about science. Compared to youngsters in other advanced nations, American students consistently score close to the bottom in tests of scientific achievement."[8]

I would suggest three goals that should be part of science education. The first is to encourage students to give serious consideration to a career in science. This is best done by helping them to experience the excitement of uncovering new truths and comprehending how something, whether organic or inorganic, works. Most children have a sense of wonder about nature. The successful secondary science teacher helps students recapture that feeling of awe. Laboratory work is a very productive means of developing interest in science. However, it is important that experiments not be merely "cookbook recipes" in which the student follows precise directions to reach a predetermined result. When full directions about equipment and procedures, as well as solutions, are provided, there is no opportunity for the independence of thinking that makes science challenging and fun.

This leads to the second goal for the science teacher: to develop in all students the sort of thinking that makes up the scientific method. Obviously, scientific thinking is essential for those who are going on in science, but it is also important for those who will pursue other fields because it will give them intellectual skills that they can apply to a wide range of areas. Science trains students to be nonjudgmental and to avoid wishful thinking since scientists must accept the facts as they are. Science trains students in observation so that they can determine what the facts are. Science strengthens the ability to analyze those facts and draw conclusions from the analysis. Finally, and most important, science trains students in the ability to ask the pertinent questions and to follow the answers wherever they may lead.

The third essential element of science education is to train citizens to understand and evaluate the results of scientific discovery. Secondary students who are going on to university should at the very least be able to comprehend a newspaper article about science. This basic knowledge is essential if one is to be a literate person in the twenty-first century. It is also important because as voters or persons in positions of decision-making, nonscientists often have to make judgments that will affect science or require the knowledge of science. For example, recently the British House of Commons had a free vote on abortion. This means that each member was allowed to vote with his conscience rather than follow the dictates of the Party Whips. The members of Parliament, who are mostly lawyers and businessmen, had to understand the basic biology of fetal development in order to vote wisely.

Of course, the most important area of science that everyone should understand is biology, especially issues relating to human health. The ability to ask probing questions of the medical profession and to make judgments about environmental matters is important for everyone. For this reason, I believe that subjects traditionally taught in "health" courses should be taught in biology. These include such matters as sexuality, nutrition, and disease prevention. By teaching these subjects as part of the regular biological offerings, a curriculum emphasizes the seriousness of these matters and helps turn the subject matter of biology from merely theoretical to one having a direct impact on the lives of the students.

Our Small World

The sixth area that a secondary school curriculum should address is our ever-shrinking world. Obviously, communication is of vital importance and competence in a foreign language is an essential ingredient of a curriculum. It is important to remember that foreign language study not only allows for communication, but also helps in understanding the thought patterns and world views of another people. While I have argued earlier for a grounding in one's own culture, a good curriculum also provides for knowledge of foreign history and culture.

Here I would argue that depth is more important than breadth. It is unlikely that even a broad program of world history and culture will be able to cover all the varieties of experience that make up human life. By studying one particular history and culture deeply, a student may learn to appreciate and empathize with those people being examined. If he is able to do this in one foreign culture, he is much more likely to be able to do so with other peoples. A superficial understanding of many cultures rarely develops this sensitivity.

Finally, many studies have shown that American students are woefully lacking in knowledge of geography. Geography includes both the location of places on a map and an understanding of the climate and resources of those places. Whether geography is taught as a separate subject or whether it is made an essential part of other social science areas, it is very important that American students significantly improve their knowledge of the rest of the world.

The Arts

The arts, in the broad sense of the word, include music, drama, fine arts, and crafts. They make up the seventh element I would propose for a curriculum. Here I would make the goal to be the development of appreciative and critical skills in students so that they become more sophisticated audiences for the arts. Sometimes, these skills are best taught in courses which stress appreciation and history of the arts, but they are also developed by participation and hands-on experience. The ability to recognize excellence in the arts not only helps define an educated person, it also enriches that person's life by developing his or her aesthetic sense. This in turn helps the arts because a critical audience demands a higher level of performance from the artist.

Decision-Making

The last two aspects of the curriculum I would stress are ones that are not usually taught in secondary school. I believe that we will ill prepare those who are students in the 1990s if we do not attempt to train them in these areas. The eighth aspect is training in decision-making. As the number of options open to a person and therefore the number of choices he or she must make continue to grow, schools should give serious thought to helping train students in this skill. During the rapid changes of the 1960s, many schools offered their students more choices about lifestyle, appearance, and course selection in the belief that by allowing students to make choices, they were helping to train them in decision-making. It is probably true that one best learns about making choices when one has to bear the responsibility for those choices. However, it is also a tenet of American graduate professional schools that one can learn to make decisions in theoretical and hypothetical situations. The case study method of the business schools is the best example, but theoretical decision-making is also used to some extent in law, medical and other schools. I believe that secondary schools could learn from the graduate schools and help train students in decision-making through the case method.

Although the distinction might not always be a clear one, students should be trained in two types of decisions. The first I would call practical and would include such things as college selection and career decisions. Perhaps some discussion of what to look for in a spouse might reduce the drastic failure rate of so many people in this area. The case method can also be used to help students develop moral reasoning. I will speak more of training in ethical decision-making in the next chapter.

Visual Communication

The final ingredient of a curriculum I consider essential is visual communication. I remember speaking with the faculty of a boarding school in 1977 and saying how important I thought it was to train students in the uses and abuses of television. A teacher raised his hand and said, "Oh, you believe in fad education." I shook my head and said: "If you think television is a passing fad then you and I have such a different view of the modern world that it is unlikely that we will ever reach agreement." In 1988, the ABC television network was claiming that more people got their news from ABC than from any other source. Certainly in the presidential election of 1988 it was obvious that each candidate was trying to come up with the witty quip or be photographed in the right situation to capture a minute or two on the evening news rather than explain in depth what he would do about various issues if he were president. The power of the visual is so immense in our society that it seems to me unwise for schools to put all their emphasis on the use and analysis of the written word and to neglect visual communication. Students should be given more opportunities to learn from the visual, but it is even more important that they learn how visual communication affects them and their world. The arrival of the hand-held VCR camera makes it possible for them not only to study visual communication, but also to have the experience of producing it.

What the Curriculum Would Produce

As one thinks about matters of curriculum, one should keep in mind the sort of adult we wish the curriculum to produce. I am reminded of an English headmaster who was showing a young boy around the school. He showed him the magnificent Gothic buildings which had been solidly standing there for centuries. He showed him the wonderful green lawns and playing fields, the beautiful gardens, the lists of graduates who had gone off to distinction and service of the Empire, and he turned to the boy and said: "Never, never suppose for a moment that all of this exists simply so that you can get a better job." Nelson Rockefeller said something somewhat similar at a graduation address at Syracuse University: "Have you spent four years here so that your local doctor may have you as his most affluent ulcer patient?"[9]

Teachers

I believe very strongly that there is an element in schools that is of considerably more importance than the formal curriculum. Of course, I am referring to the teachers. Their ability, enthusiasm, and care for students will be the most critical factors in determining the degree to which their students become educated adults. While it is not my purpose to write at length about teachers, I would like to make several comments about them.

America is facing not only a shortage of teachers, but an even more drastic decline in the quality of teachers. At most universities, those entering freshmen who indicate they intend to have a career in primary or secondary education have median SAT scores lower than almost any other academic discipline. Part of this, of course, is because of the low pay and low prestige traditionally associated with noncollegiate teaching, but there is another significant factor. Until fairly recently, teaching was one of the few professions readily open to women and minorities. Today, as other professions have opened up, the most talented women and minority students are drawn away from teaching, thus leaving the field to those without the talent to pursue other careers, or to those with very strong dedication. If America continues to entrust its most precious resource, its children, to the least talented of university graduates, we can hardly expect to have the educated population that is necessary for national strength in the twenty-first century.

If we are to attract people of quality to teaching, then they must be regarded as professionals. And if teachers are to *be* professionals, they need to be treated as such. Professionals in other vocations are given considerable freedom in how they conduct their professional lives and then are held accountable for the results. Sadly, this is frequently not the case in education. In some states, central boards of education determine what books shall be read in all classrooms. In other areas, those determinations are made by a local school board. In many schools, teachers must submit detailed lesson plans for advance approval by school authorities. These controls rob a teacher of the independence to make professional judgments about what is best for his or her students. On the other hand, teachers are rarely judged by the results they get, and as long as they do not rock the boat too much, they can be assured of a secure tenure. In fact, when cuts in faculty have to be made, they are often made on the basis of seniority, not quality. Many schools operate with a system in which the administration tries to tell the teachers in advance what to do but then provides little quality control over what they actually do accomplish. This seems to me the exact opposite of how to attract and retain a professional faculty.

Teachers are participating in the modern American trend of changing employers with some frequency, and increasingly of changing careers. This means that we are seeing a number of young people enter teaching for a few years and then go on other occupations. We are also seeing more experienced teachers move from school to school. While in some cases this brings new ideas into a school, it also means that longtime institutional loyalty and close association between teachers and graduates are likely to decline.

It is important to remember that teaching is an art that cannot be systematized. Like most arts, greatness in teaching is usually obvious when it is present, but what makes it great is often hard to define. Teaching skills can be taught and they can be improved. However, the ability to ignite that magic chemistry between teacher and student has an elusive quality that is hard to pin down in a set of instructions or even a theory. John Rae, Headmaster of London's Westminster School, writes:

"How can a theory do justice to the variety of responses to a particular teacher—scorned by some of his pupils, admired by others—or to the disconcerting truth, that where a conscientious teacher makes little impression, a self-centred, inflexible man whose idiosyncrasies border on the insane, can inspire his pupils with deep and lasting love of his subject. Education theory does not, indeed cannot, account for such peculiarities."[10]

On this side of the Atlantic, Howard Means writes that great schools are made up of faculties that are "bedlams of eccentricity."[11]

Sometimes a little eccentricity on the part of the principal or headmaster is also not misplaced. I am a Halloween junkie and every year I devise a new outlandish costume. I arrive at school in my regular clothing and make sure that most people see me. Then I make a quick change in my office and go around the school, barging into classrooms and being as disruptive as possible. It is my hope that the teachers will think I am a troublesome twelfth grader. Unfortunately, by now all the old hands know who I am, as do most of the students. Fortunately, they rarely warn the new teachers. I remember recently bursting into the classroom of a very young and very earnest mathematics teacher who was in his first job. He took one look at the gruesome monster who was disturbing his lesson and shouted at the top of his voice: "Damn it! Get the hell out of here!" As I beat a hasty retreat, I could hear the students saying with great glee, "Do you know who that was?" Of course, when he came to apologize, I told him he had been absolutely right to defend his classroom and make sure that nothing interrupted his work. The tables were turned on me one year when I was glomping in my costume through the hallways and spotted the Assistant Headmaster showing a group of four distinguished German educators around the school. I thought I would slip by them, but the Assistant Headmaster stopped me and introduced our guests to the slightly eccentric headmaster of St. Albans. I hate to think what they reported back to Germany about American education.

One of the problems of American education has been that certification requirements for schools have put more emphasis on a teacher's credentials than on his personality. I was pleased to hear the Dean of the Leningrad Pedagogical University tell American educators that teachers must be "interesting people for their students." Although his university is a major source granting credentials for teachers and principals, he recognizes that credentials do not necessarily produce the sort of chemistry that makes for exciting education.

There is always a danger that either school administrators or parents will prefer order, structure, and conformity to what is exciting, unrehearsed, and challenging. As Patrick Welsh puts it in *Tales Out of School:*

"Teaching methods that give us such things as the sponge activity are in an old tradition of schooling that holds that 'the quiet child is a good child.' The goal seems to be a risk-free environment—one in which classes never get out of hand, subjects taught do not threaten or offend students, and grading is 'in line' with normal curves. But risk and spontaneity are at the heart of learning. The best moments in my class are frequently those that are totally unprepared—when, for one reason or another, my students take me in an unexpected direction. A sense of humor is one of a teacher's assets. But you won't find the new literature on 'effective teaching' dwelling much on the need for fun and spontaneity in the classroom. The longer I teach, the more determined I am to combat passivity. Teaching often involves an element of trickery—the purpose being to 'trick' kids into suspending the 'game' long enough to let their natural curiosity and enthusiasm come out. Words such as 'delight,' 'humor,' 'surprise,' and 'feelings' ought to be part of an educator's vocabulary now more than ever."[12]

As I think about my own teaching and that of my colleagues, two tendencies concern me most. We are quicker to criticize and point out shortcomings than we are to praise and encourage. Yet I believe that human beings respond more to positive reinforcement than they do to the negative. At one time I was a dean at a large boarding school. To overcome the lack of communication caused by the size of the school, a system of comment cards was instituted. Whenever a faculty member had something to say about a student, whether in or out of class, he or she was to write a comment card, one copy of which would go to the student's adviser and the other to the dean. This was a leading boarding school with very fine students who went on to the most selective colleges. Yet to read the comment cards, one would have thought it was a detention camp for juvenile delinquents. Ninety percent of the comment cards were about something a student had done wrong or an obligation not met. Only a few offered any praise for the many wonderful accomplishments of our students.

I think we as teachers also fail to communicate with parents frequently enough. Parents who love their children like to hear about them. Obviously, they like to hear good news rather than bad, but the conscientious parent appreciates the bad news so that he or she can move on the situation before it gets worse. Certainly as a parent, I find myself correcting my children more than I like to. When a teacher tells me something good about one of them, it gives me an opportunity to pass on the word of praise and add my own appreciation.

My other concern as a teacher is that our present educational system puts so much emphasis on individual accomplishment while our students are growing up into a world where the ability to cooperate and work well with others will be of extreme importance. Both our instructional methods and, even more, our testing methods stress what the individual student can accomplish. It is hard to devise educational projects that are done by a team. Too often it means that one student does most of the work and the others share in the credit. But educators must recognize that in most of the professional world, let alone in one's own personal life, tasks are accomplished by teamwork and group activity. New methods must be found to prepare our students for the cooperation needed in adulthood.

Somewhat similar concerns were apparent in the 1990 Assessment Seminars conducted by Richard J. Light. Nearly four hundred undergraduates at Harvard were surveyed about what they found most valuable in their courses. The crucial features were

"immediate and detailed feedback on both written and oral work; high demands and standards placed upon them, with plentiful opportunities to revise and improve their work before it receives a grade, thereby learning from their mistakes in the process; and frequent checkpoints, such as quizzes, tests, brief papers or oral exams. The key idea is that most students feel they learn best when they receive frequent evaluation, combined with the opportunity to revise their work and improve it over time. Early evidence suggests that students who work in small groups, even when interacting with high-tech equipment, learn significantly more than students who work primarily alone. In every comparison of how much students learn when they work in small groups with how much they learn either in large groups or when they work alone, small groups show the best outcomes."[13]

My final word on teaching is directed to those who entrust children to teachers, or those who presume to administer schools. In some ways teaching is a lonely profession. Teachers normally spend their days without allies in the classroom and are greatly outnumbered by their adversaries. In the English and Japanese systems, in which external examinations are all important, the students are not necessarily adversaries of the teacher. The external examiner becomes the foe. In a system where the same person must be both the imparter of wisdom and then the final judge of how much wisdom was imparted, and where the person then gives the grade that goes on the college transcript, there is naturally somewhat of an adversarial relationship. Great teachers are able both to exploit that relationship so that their students achieve maximum results and to overcome that relationship so that there is a lasting bond of mutual affection and respect between teacher and student. To function successfully with that tension of being both adversary and friend is a difficult role indeed. The difficulty is even greater because of the lack of rewards a teacher receives. The lack of financial reward is so obvious that it need not be mentioned, but there is also a lack of status in our society. Many teachers report to me that when they see a college classmate and indicate that they are teaching, the classmate comes close to asking, "What are you going to do when you grow up?"

Because teaching is a solitary activity, and because when students have success it is right that they should get the credit, teachers receive little praise. To parents and administrators I would say most vigorously: if you want to have good teachers, be sure to praise them any time you find an opportunity. To teachers, I would say: you will have to be content with these words from Robert Bolt's *A Man for All Seasons.* Thomas More advises Richard Rich to give up politics and go into teaching, suggesting that Rich could be a great teacher: "And if I was, who would know it?" asks Rich. More replies, "You, your pupils, your friends, God. Not a bad public, that. . . ."[14]

Chapter Six

All Good Works

As I begin to consider the teaching of morality in the secondary schools, I would like to note two aspects of the problem. First, it is a problem that has confronted every generation as it tries to instruct its young. Frequently, adults become very discouraged and believe that the young are headed for almost certain disaster. Examples abound throughout history—from the classical and biblical periods through the Middle Ages, the Renaissance, and into modern times. Such examples should be cautionary for all of us concerned with the young. Each generation has its deep doubts about the morals of those who will follow. Our parents worried about us and it is easy for us to believe that our students are lost in a moral wilderness.

The second aspect worth mentioning is that in America in the early 1990s, most bands of the cultural spectrum are calling for a greater emphasis on morality. Of course, those different groups do not agree on what aspects should be stressed. Ronald Reagan and other conservatives called for a greater emphasis on personal ethics. He told the convention of the National Association of Independent Schools that failure to teach morality was the public's greatest complaint about schools. At the other end of the spectrum, when I told a friend who teaches Marxist philosophy that I would spend some of my sabbatical thinking and writing about the teaching of ethics, he replied: "We certainly need a book on that. None of us knows how to do it effectively." And in the mainstream of American life, *Time* magazine has run cover stories and articles on the crisis of ethics.[1] While some of this must be attributed to the fear adults have about the next generation, the rapid changes in American life during the last half of this century have produced significant new challenges for the teaching of ethics. Before we look at these, I want to identify five ways that morality has been taught and ethical behavior encouraged.

Teaching Morality

First, and probably oldest, has been a system of rewards and punishments: "If you hit your baby brother, I'll spank you" or "If you stop crying, I'll give you a piece of candy." An appeal to the mystical can be made to older children. An American Indian mother may have said: "If you aren't good, the evil spirit of the north woods will steal you away." Modern Americans hear over department store sound systems a warning: "Santa Claus is coming to town. He knows if you've been naughty. He knows if you've been nice. He knows if you've been bad or good, so be good for goodness' sake."

Of course, there is a major problem with a morality that is based on rewards and punishments. It is soon clear to any observer that the good are not always rewarded and the evil not always punished. Therefore, the compensation is frequently moved to another life. For Christians and Moslems, heaven and hell provide the promise of just rewards and punishments so often missing in this life.

Who could gaze at the wall of the Sistine Chapel without grasping Michelangelo's view of what awaited evildoers?

Clearly, rewards and punishments are one of the principal ways of training young children to behave in the desired way. For adolescents, this is much less effective. Part of the process of separating from parents involves a certain amount of risk-taking, testing both one's own courage and the elasticity of rules and limits set down by others. Moreover, adolescents vary in the rate in which they develop the ability to postpone present gratification for future satisfaction. Therefore, rewards or punishments that are too far in the future are usually not effective. Finally, there is a dark side to adolescents that can only be described as a potential for self-destruction. They do have a high suicide rate. Even those who never come near to doing themselves physical harm often have a sort of martyr complex. They are willing to forgo their own best interest for the sake of some personal principle or to assert their independence. Thus, the appeal to self-interest involved in a system of rewards and punishments often falls on deaf ears.

The second method used to encourage good behavior is to appeal to the human instinct to conform. While all of us like to think of ourselves as individuals, few of us like to be too different from those around us. In primitive societies, the power of the taboo was great. In more civilized societies the words "That sort of thing just isn't done" have at times been effective controllers of behavior. Such appeals work best in a small group or a highly homogeneous society. It is not surprising that two island nations, England and Japan, both relatively isolated, developed this sort of moral sanction to a high degree. In a country such as the United States, whose society is becoming more and more diverse, it has little effectiveness.

It is clear that adolescents often enjoy violating the

conformity that adults try to impose on them, but they are eager to conform to the standards of other teenagers. Thus, when peer pressure can be directed toward the good, it may be a powerful force in moral education. Frequently, however, it works in the opposite direction.

Control of behavior is most powerful when it moves from mere conformity to a response to a personal relationship. The desire to please, or serve a particular person or persons about whom one cares, is a most potent controller of behavior. When I am looking over my ten-year-old son's schoolwork, he is not particularly interested in what he has accomplished, but he sometimes asks me, "Will you be angry if I get it wrong?" That question is natural in a child of that age because pleasing his parents is so very important to him.

The finest actions of an adult are usually based on personal relationships. The selfless devotion of a mother toward a sick child is an obvious example. Similarly, most men who display great courage in battle report afterwards that abstract terms such as patriotism or democracy were not in their minds, but a desire to save their buddies on the battlefield. It has been my experience that secondary school students get themselves in the deepest difficulties when they are trying either to impress their friends or to protect them. Christianity, which has had such an overwhelming influence on the morality of this country, stresses that, at its highest, morality is not a matter of following rules, but of being in a personal relationship with God and pleasing Him.

The fourth way of inculcating morality is to stress duty. Sometimes the duty is claimed simply by being alive or being born in a particular country: "You have an obligation to help those less fortunate than yourself" or "Every person has a duty to defend his country when it is attacked." More often, the duty is stressed because of a commitment or involvement a person has: "Every student in this school has an obligation to represent the school well in public" or "You have a duty as a husband to be faithful to your wife" or "You signed a contract and therefore must fulfill your part of the bargain."

Finally, I believe that the most powerful teacher of ethics is example. Albert Schweitzer put it strongly: "Example is not the most important way of teaching morality; it is the only way." All of us who are parents are painfully aware of the fact that sometimes the examples we set override the teachings we give our children. If teaching morality by example is difficult for us as parents, it is even more difficult for schools. The legal system and changes in societal attitudes have made it an extremely risky business for schools to impose too much on the personal and moral lives of faculty members. As there is less and less consensus about what constitutes the moral norms in this country, it is harder to expect teachers to conform to any particular set of principles. Even when teachers violate generally accepted norms, they are now frequently protected by legal defenses.

I am both sympathetic and critical of the president of a large university who spoke to a reunioning group of alumni a few years ago. He told them it was imperative that universities encourage moral thinking and moral action in students. The next day the campus carried an article about a professor who had been arrested for beating up his girlfriend. The article ended with an inverview with the university president who was aksed if the man would be dismissed. The president replied: "What he does in his personal life is a matter for him and the courts to resolve. At this university he will be judged on his professional competency." I understand the legal constraints that were on that president, but I also find it difficult to see how he could talk about moral education for the young and keep on the faculty a man who so flagrantly violated any standard of decent behavior.

As we think about moral education through example, it is helpful to remember the examples being held in front of our students today. I believe that it is good that the press takes a vigorous role in ferreting out wrongdoing by people in positions of public trust and responsibility. However, because those examples of wrongdoing are so often before the young, it is a very challenging task to encourage them to behave in other ways. They are inundated with examples of lying, putting self-interest above the needs of others, attacking others through innuendo and rumor, and blatant cheating. Young people learn early that such activities are carried out by people whom our society admires and rewards disproportionately. It has probably always been thus, but more probing press corps and television news teams make young people more aware of these examples than they were in the past.

Forces That Shape Morality

I believe that the problem of inculcating morality today has developed because one of the three forces that have traditionally shaped values in America has become dominant over the other two. The first force was religion. Many of the early settlers in America came for religious reasons, and religion played a major role in the shaping of society. As the society has become increasingly secular during the twentieth century, the power of religion as a teacher of morality has drastically declined. Moreover, the very plurality of cultures and religions of which Americans are so proud, makes it unlikely that values of any one religion will be acceptable to the whole society. The major exception to these trends, of course, has been the rapid growth of fundamentalism in the last twenty years. Fundamentalists tend to agree on most moral teachings. Not only do they demand that their followers obey such teachings, they also try to impose them on society as a whole. In fact, it is often reaction to such attempts to control others that makes nonfundamentalists even more cautious about using religion as a basis for teaching values.

The second force has been the power of the community. In a rural area or a small village in which people not only knew everyone else, but were often highly dependent on each other, there was less need for the schools to teach values. The community usually agreed on values, taught them to the children, and then through community pressure insisted on compliance. Often this resulted in narrowness or bigotry, but it did provide an effective moral structure. In America in the last half of this century, not only do most Americans live in urban areas, but they are highly mobile and will live in several different urban areas over the course of a lifetime. In our complex society we are, in a way, even more dependent on other people, but frequently those are people whose names or faces we will never know. In fact, those of us who live in urban areas sometimes find that we may know the faces but not the names of our immediate neighbors. The anonymity of modern life has removed the community as an effective force in inculcating and enforcing morality.

The third force, which I believe has risen to prominence with the decline of the other two, is the philosophical notion of liberalism. Its most influential advocate was John Locke.[2] It is ironic that he wrote to defend the glorious revolution of 1688, which placed William on the throne of England, but his words and thoughts had their greatest impact on the founders of the American republic. His political influence is readily obvious. Locke wrote that every individual has a right to "life, liberty, and assets."

He believed that the purpose of government was to ensure those rights. He thought that the best way to avoid tyranny was to separate the executive and legislative function of government. He even proposed a three-way separation of power. His proposed third branch of the government was not the judicial, but what he called the federative, which was to deal with foreign affairs. Most important, he believed that it was possible and sometimes necessary to change a government, and that one could do so without destroying society and slipping into anarchy. We take that notion almost for granted, but it is relatively new in human history, and still not accepted in much of the world today.

Locke's political ideas are most familiar to and influential on Americans. His philosophical ideas are of equal importance in the development of the American sense of morality. Locke believed that men are born "like a white piece of paper, with no innate ideas." All that we know comes to us through experience, either through the sensations or through our reasoning. This means that we do not have an inborn sense of right and wrong, or of obligations and duty. We develop those as we grow. Moreover, not only are we lacking in innate ideas, but we are born in what Locke calls a state of nature. In a state of nature each individual is free. He has no necessary connections with other people. His reason will tell him he must respect the freedom of others if he is to be free. Therefore, he can do whatever he wants as long as he does not infringe on the life, liberty, or property of others. Unfortunately, sometimes people do impose on others, and therefore, reason leads man to form, through social contracts, first a society and then a government. In this way, life, liberty, and property may be protected. The important point here is that the reason for entering into the social contract, for surrendering some of one's liberties, and for accepting obligations is essentially self-interest.

I believe that the modern American position of morality is essentially Lockean. The modern American believes he has a right to use his own mind to determine moral positions. He does not receive and accept the edicts of the church or community or even his parents. The modern American believes he should be free to do what he wants ("pursue his own lifestyle") as long as he does not hurt anyone else. He does not believe that such abstractions as truth, justice, and duty are floating out there at the mouth of a Platonic cave. Rather, they are socially useful ideals, which may be violated when another necessity presents itself. The modern American believes that he enters into commitments with others for mutual benefits and that when those benefits cease, the commitment should end. This is seen most clearly in modern attitudes toward marriage. ("She is no longer meeting my needs so I must seek a new relationship.") It is also increasingly true in matters of business and other social contracts. As the authors of *Habits of the Heart* succinctly put it:

"The expressive aspect of our culture exists for the liberation and fulfillment of the individual. Its genius is that it enables the individual to think of commitments—from marriage and work to political and religious involvement—as enhancements of the sense of individual well-being rather than as moral imperatives."[3]

One interesting twist to the Lockean view of reality is that when Locke wrote about the state of nature, Europeans were excited by the new world across the Atlantic, where human beings appeared to live in a state of nature, not bound by all the ties, obligations, and traditions of Europe. Of course, this was a gross misunderstanding of Native Americans and the tribal and religious taboos that shaped their lives. The irony is that it is in modern, secular, and urban America where human beings have come closest to the state of nature. An unmarried urban person can pursue almost any lifestyle, has almost no obligation to others other than at work, and feels little compunction about changing employment if those obligations become too onerous. I believe that the increase in popularity of fundamentalism is an attempt to escape from the isolation of the autonomous Lockean individual.

There is one other aspect of modern morality that must be mentioned. As we have put emphasis on the autonomous self rather than the moral being who is interconnected through commitments and obligations to others, our view not only of morality, but of immorality has changed. What used to be called evil or wrong or even, that most old-fashioned of words, sinful, is now described as sick or dysfunctional. Society is producing an attitude which encourages us to avoid making judgments on ourselves and others. It is not surprising that when Allan Bloom asked his students at the University of Chicago to name both heroes and evil people, few students could get beyond Adolf Hitler in composing the latter list.[4]

The Lockean view of the individual has been reflected in moral teaching in our schools. Here the emphasis has not been on right and wrong. Instead, it has become "value clarification," that is, helping each individual to determine what values he or she will hold in order to maximize self-fulfillment.

There are others who are better equipped to give a philosophical critique of Locke's position. I want merely to point out that as Lockean liberalism has become the dominant force in the thinking of all but fundamentalist Americans, and as the state of nature has become almost a reality for urban Americans, we have lost those two other forces, religion and the community, which help provide moral guidelines. By emphasizing the isolated individual whose only obligation is to maximize his or her self-fulfillment, we have lost much of the underpinnings for moral behavior. There are, however, a number of things that schools can do to help their students grow into moral beings.

Schools and Morality

Schools should be rigorous in demanding that truth is essential to the moral life. This, of course, is important for a school because the search for truth is at the heart of the academic enterprise, but schools can also insist on truth because it is so essential to moral behavior. Students can be helped to see that nothing breaks down human relationships faster or impedes communication more than a disregard for the truth. I remember an experienced headmaster saying once: "I will work with any student, with any problem, except a student who will not tell me the truth, because then I cannot effectively relate to him." Students can be shown that this statement applies in all human relationships. Schools must be vigorous in demanding not only that students are always truthful, but that faculty and administrators are as well. Of course, one of the major reasons why students violate the truth is to cover up mistakes or wrongdoing. I think that many of us in school work are guilty of imposing a sort of perfectionism on our students. We can encourage respect for the truth by helping students see that failure is an opportunity for growth, rather than a measure of their worth as human beings.

One of the reasons truth is so important is that it ties us into reality. Helping students accept and appreciate reality is very important in their moral education. Schools can help students learn that limits are the reality of the human condition. We are all limited in time, we are limited in resources, we are limited in knowledge, and we are very limited in ability to act without affecting others. Most of all, schools can show students that actions have consequences. By holding to academic standards, acknowledging positive achievement, and maintaining discipline, a school demonstrates the relationship between action and consequences. The knowledge of that relationship is essential in the process of becoming a responsible adult. As they grow in maturity, students learn that there are consequences for behavior in terms of long-range satisfaction and happiness, even if such results are not immediately apparent.

John Silber, President of Boston University, in his provocative book, *Straight Shooting*, argues that understanding reality is the most important form of moral education:

"The first objective of early education should be training in the reality principle . . . Reality provides the conditions on which pleasure can or cannot be achieved; it also provides the moral conditions on which pleasure should or should not be achieved. This value-freighted reality reveals the conditions that must be met or avoided if there is to be any gratification at any time . . . If there is to be effective moral education, it must begin in early childhood . . . If we have the courage to face reality, we will know and proclaim these harrowing truths: that the degenerate society consumed in pleasure-seeking will not survive, that the society that will not defend its freedom will lose it, that the society that consumes more than it produces will go bankrupt. We will ill serve ourselves and our children by preparing ourselves and them for a life of freedom and easy pleasure that may never come and most certainly will never last. We had better prepare ourselves and them for reality—a reality that is infused with moral laws as surely as it is infused with physical laws; a reality in which there is no consumption without production, no freedom without defense, no self-fulfillment and no self-government without self-disciplined persons who govern themselves, persons who are capable of subordinating their desires long enough to achieve the conditions on which freedom and survival, and even pleasure, depend . . . And educators should ensure that reality is packed into the curriculum so that their students, prior to graduation, will confront reality . . . These ideas should prepare young people for the disappointment that is an essential part of the joy of living. Thus, if we are to retain our joy in life, we must find much of that joy in spite of disappointment, for the joy of life consists largely in the joy of savoring the struggle, whether it ends in success or failure. Our ability to go through life successfully will depend largely upon our traveling with courage and a good sense of humor, for both are conditions of survival."[5]

I believe that the modern tendency to make commitments and honor them only when it is expedient is one of the major causes of moral confusion in our time. I would urge schools to look for ways to help students understand the importance of commitments and obligations. Most of the commitments that students make during school life are of significantly less importance than those they will make later. By insisting that they meet their obligations now, schools can train students in the habit of meeting commitments later on. One important aspect of this is helping students to understand that obligations affect others as well as themselves.

This leads to another important approach that schools can take in teaching morality. Adolescence is a time of great egocentricity. The process of moving from childhood to adulthood is so consuming that it is hard for students to think of others. Often we encourage this egocentricity because we focus so much attention on our students, and we say that our schools exist to serve them. We need also to help them understand that while the adults in the school do have an obligation to serve them, the students also have an obligation for service. As the head of a church school, I feel comfortable in telling my students that the school does not exist ultimately for them. I go on to add that it does not exist for the alumni or the parents. It exists to serve God. That line is not available to most heads of schools, but all of us can look for ways to counteract the egocentricity of adolescence which is reinforced so strongly by the youth-centered culture of modern America.

This emphasis on thinking of others should be put into practical terms. A well-developed social service program will give students both an exposure to the needs of others and an opportunity to express their concern in practical terms. Some schools will have a voluntary program whereas others will require participation. All should encourage social service and make it a high priority for the use of school resources and time. To talk of morality and not provide opportunities to put compassion for others into practice is self-defeating.

The Madeira School in northern Virginia goes so far as to take one day a week off classes to allow students lengthy and meaningful experiences of social service on and off campus. By stopping all other school activities on that day, social service becomes not only a way of serving others but very much a shared experience for the students in the school.

All human beings relish an opportunity to be helpful to others, and the young particularly need the experience. Many students report that the opportunity to be of help to others was the most meaningful part of their secondary school experience. John FitzGerald, a recent graduate of the Landon School in Bethesda, has written: "My four-year participation in community service has been my most meaningful experience. I have lead support groups at Landon and worked with area teenagers in the Red Cross Coping With Alcohol Program. Early in my Senior year I joined nine other peer counselors to develop a teenage suicide awareness program for the Mental Health Association. We called the program 'LIFE', Living Is For Everyone. It was exciting to see the impact of the program on audiences when we presented it during the year to area schools and other groups. I plan to continue in similar programs next year at the University of Virginia."

The classroom is another place where a school can demand moral thinking and decision-making. If we can teach business or law students to make decisions through the case method, we can also teach ethical decision-making. Any experienced school person will have a backlog of real-life examples of moral dilemmas in which students find themselves. The use of these as cases for discussion can be quite effective. Moreover, cases that involve more adult problems such as marriage or business ethics can help students think beyond their own immediate situation and learn to face problems they will meet in the future. Courses in moral thinking cannot provide the will to do what is right, but they can help students think more clearly and make more effective moral decisions in a highly complex world.

Sometimes a class discussion can move from the theoretical to the particular. I remember very interesting discussions with some eighth grade students in 1984. They were asked to be among the first juveniles arrested in front of the South African Embassy for protesting apartheid. I like to think it was educational for both them and me to talk about the issues of when it is correct to break the law (in this case, the law against protesting within a certain number of feet in front of an embassy), and the effects of that protest on the South African government, the boys' consciences, and their futures.

Most important, schools must always be conscious that their clearest moral teaching will be by example. The way faculty and administrators treat each other and students, the regard held for truth, what student misbehavior is punished and what is ignored, what student accomplishment is publicly praised and honored, and the moral life of each adult in the community will have an enormous impact on the students. Developing a moral climate in a school is a tremendously difficult task for school leaders, but if there is to be any effective moral education in a school, it must be among the highest priorities for that school.

A Personal Example

I close this chapter on the teaching of morality with a painful example from St. Albans School. I share the example with some reluctance because to relate it is to tell of a success and I do not want to use these pages to boast. I probably am guilty of some pride, but I tell the story to illustrate how one school engaged in moral teaching. For several years, St. Albans did nothing about AIDS education. I suppose we hoped that it was a danger overestimated by the press or perhaps that it was a problem that would happen to another school first. By the academic year 1986–87, we became convinced that it was a serious national problem. We instituted a program of AIDS education through the biology department because we thought the approach should be scientific and factual. Because we had not acted in the past, the biology teachers had a short mini-course with those students who had already taken biology. We had the author of a book on AIDS speak to the whole school and invited all parents to attend that lecture. We sent a copy of the Surgeon General's report on AIDS to all parents and urged them to discuss it with their children. The Governing Board approved a policy on communicable diseases which called for the creation of a committee whenever the school became aware that a student or faculty member had a communicable disease.

The day before classes were to begin in September 1987, the classics teacher of St. Albans School told me that he had been diagnosed as having Acquired Immune Deficiency Syndrome. In accordance with our communicable disease policy, a committee began to consider the situation. The committee was chaired by the school's consulting physician. It included trustees, parents, alumni, and faculty representatives. We were aware that other schools had had a teacher with AIDS and had asked the teacher to resign, while others had kept the matter quiet. We did not know of any school that had informed its parents that it was keeping a teacher with AIDS in the classroom. We also knew that one month earlier the Florida home of young children with AIDS had been burned down in an attempt to drive the children from the public schools.

In close consultation with our classics teacher, the decision was made to inform the school family of his situation and to have him remain in the classroom. I informed the faculty, staff, and students in meetings and sent a letter to all parents (see pages 132 and 133).

I had over two hundred written responses to my letter and did not keep track of the large number of people who spoke to me in person. Only three parents expressed any reservation about our actions and no one withdrew from either the afflicted teacher's classes or the school. It was obvious that some students were nervous about the situa-

St. Albans School

Mount St. Alban
Washington, D.C. 20016

Headmaster's Study October 6, 1987

Dear Parents:

Last year the Governing Boards of the Cathedral Schools adopted a policy on communicable diseases which was then approved by the Cathedral Chapter. It called for the establishment of a committee to consider, on an individual basis, any case of communicable disease among students or employees of the Cathedral schools. The policy indicated that the committee should consist of physicians, members of the Governing Board, and other representatives of the School family.

Tragically, that committee had to be called into being at the beginning of this academic year and has met frequently during the past three weeks. At his request, I write to tell you that Mr. Vaughn Keith, Classics teacher at St. Albans, has been diagonosed as having Acquired Immune Deficiency Syndrome. The School's physician has discussed the situation carefully with both Mr. Keith and his doctor. All of the medical evidence, including the Surgeon General's Report which many of you read last year, indicates that this illness cannot be transmitted by casual contact. The laws of the District of Columbia are also quite clear. A person may not be denied employment because he is diagnosed as having AIDS. It is not, however, mandated by law that parents in a school be informed if a teacher has AIDS. In fact, some schools or districts have exactly the opposite policy.

Mr. Keith and the School want you to know about his illness for two reasons. First, not only fairness to you as parents, but honesty and integrity demand openness. The second reason is even more important. If medical predictions about the course of this disease in our society hold true, there is no question that within the next five to ten years, our sons will have other teachers, friends, or family members who develop this disease. Some of them may even develop it themselves. We believe that it is better

Page 2

for them to learn to respond to victims of the disease in the caring and educational community that is St. Albans than having to do so in other circumstances later in life. We will do everything possible to help our students work through their own questions and concern about this disease with a broad program of AIDS education.

Obviously, a letter like this must cause sadness and perhaps even some fear for all of us who care about our sons and Mr. Keith. But distressing as such news is, it also presents an opportunity to help our boys learn to protect themselves, to understand this disease, and to grow in their ability to respond to those who have been stricken. I admire and applaud Mr. Keith's desire to help our sons prepare themselves for a world where AIDS cases may become quite common.

How we all respond to this situation is very much a measure of St. Albans School and each of us as individuals. I ask your prayers for Mr. Keith, for St. Albans School, and for our students that God may use this tragic situation as a vehicle for growth in understanding and compassion.

Sincerely yours,

Mark H. Mullin

Mark H. Mullin
Headmaster

tion, but the vast majority made it clear that such fears were groundless. In fact, the most heartening response was from the many students who asked me about the danger of coming to class with a cold: "My teacher will have no immunity. I do not want to do anything to endanger him."

The story was picked up by the news media, including several television stations. In April, an article in *The Washington Post* reported that the Office of Personnel Management of the federal government was changing its attitudes toward AIDS, "because the director of the Office had been influenced by her son's Latin teacher." I had several letters from people not connected with the school saying that someone close to them had AIDS and how much it meant to them to have the school take a public stand.

Perhaps most moving has been what happened to the classics teacher. He saw a purpose to his suffering. He influenced so many people, not only at our school, but throughout the country and the world. Because he had a purpose in life, he was able to teach for two and a half more years before succumbing to his disease. No student who was at St. Albans during those years will forget his example.

There are a number of lessons to be learned from our experience. First, education can provide information, but it also can change how people think about moral situations. I believe we would have had quite a different reaction from our students and parents if this had occurred before we had provided education on AIDS. Second, we all know that adolescent peer pressure can be a very powerful force. In this case it was a force for good. The fears of some were overshadowed by the moral strength of the group. Third, honesty is a major component of morality. By being straightforward with our parents and students and appealing to their better motives, we enlisted their active support.

Fourth, example is the best teacher. Our example has been helpful to other schools and institutions and, most of all, to our students. Some time afterwards, a student came up to me and said: "I've heard you and others at the school talk so often about morality. It was good to see that you really mean it."

Chapter Seven

Opportunities, Dangers, and Adversities

In the previous chapters I have written about concerns that face anyone, teacher or parent, who cares about secondary school education. I want to turn now to several issues that have been of particular interest recently at my own school, St. Albans. It is clear that some of these topics are also being wrestled with at other schools and at colleges. Some, such as single-sex education or the church school, will have application only at particular schools. In this chapter I will take the liberty of discussing the issues from the St. Albans experience and leave it to the reader to relate it to his or her own situation.

Student Publications

In the fall of 1988, a very serious act of vandalism was committed in a residential area on a Saturday night. For two days rumors circulated around St. Albans that one of our students had been involved, and the Dean of Students asked some students to try to find out what had happened. On the Tuesday evening after the incident, a prominent Washington family, who happened to be friends of mine, called me and asked me to come to their home. They told me that their son, a senior at St. Albans, had committed the vandalism. We talked for a while and then the father told me that he was withdrawing his son from St. Albans immediately. He also told me that the police were aware of his son's actions and that restitution would be made for the damage.

Later that week, the Senior Prefect (the highest elected official in the senior class) charged two other seniors with violating the Honor Code in what they had said to the Dean of Students about the incident. The Honor Committee, made up of students and faculty, met and both boys were judged to be innocent of any wrongdoing.

Some time later, the faculty adviser to the student newspaper, *The St. Albans News,* came to me to ask if it would be all right to print the name of the boy who had committed the vandalism and withdrawn from school, and the two boys who had been exonerated by the Honor Committee. The faculty adviser had been a teacher at St. Albans for several years, but this was his first experience being adviser to *The News.* I told him that *The News* should not print the names of students because almost all of them were minors. I was also surprised because this was the first instance I could remember that *The News* had wanted to give a detailed description of a disciplinary matter.

The adviser asked if I would like to see the mock-up of the next edition of *The News* before it went to press. When he brought it to me, I was concerned that the article on the vandalism was so specific. Although the boy's name was not used, it was pretty clear who was involved. I was even more distressed to see that the traditional picture of the newly elected members of the Cum Laude Society had the members posing in their underwear.

I decided to meet with the entire editorial board of *The*

News to help explain to them what I expected from the publication that bore the name St. Albans. I met with the ten or so editors one afternoon. I began the meeting by saying: "I did not call you all in here to talk about the silly business about the Cum Laude Society in its underwear. Obviously, that is unfitting for the highest academic group at St. Albans School and we can't run that kind of picture. But what I would like to talk to you about is the question of how to handle the issue of student misbehavior and discipline."

To my surprise, several of the editors vigorously defended the Cum Laude photograph and thought that if the members of Cum Laude voluntarily chose to have the photograph taken in that fashion, *The News* should have the right to run it. By the time we moved on to the serious matter of the article on student discipline, it was clear that we were not going to have a meeting in which we would mutually seek to find what is the best for St. Albans and the boy who was in trouble. The issue had become that of the students' desire to publish whatever they wanted versus my desire to maintain the decency of the paper. When I pointed out to them that not only did the paper use the name St. Albans, which did not belong to the students, but that it was subsidized by the school, produced on school equipment, and distributed at the school, their response was, "Well, I guess that gives you the power to call the shots." On the issue of the boy withdrawing from school, I had said that if they wanted to run a general article about the problem of off-campus behavior, that would certainly be acceptable, but it was not permissible to write an in-depth article about one individual's disciplinary problems. The student editor replied that there would not be time to produce such an article before the publication deadline and so he would probably kill the whole thing.

Several weeks later when it was time for the next edition of *The News* to be printed, the faculty adviser again brought me mock-up. This time I discovered several articles in which slang expressions for sexual organs and drug paraphernalia had been worked into articles in ways that might appear innocent. Moreover, there was an article about a meeting I had had with the eleventh grade parents. At that meeting, several parents had criticized a particular teacher but several other parents had praised him. The article reported the criticism but made no mention of the praise. I met with the student editors again and said that sexual and drug innuendoes were not appropriate in a St. Albans publication and that in a small community, the newspaper would not be allowed to print an attack on an individual teacher. That would be too destructive of relationships within the school. I did say that the paper was free to criticize policy, but not particular individuals.

It was clear in that meeting that we were getting no closer to cooperation, and it seemed to me that it was an inappropriate role for the headmaster to be looking over mock-ups of a paper before it was printed. I had done it on two occasions because the faculty adviser had asked me to do so, but I certainly did not want to continue in that role. Therefore, I created a faculty board made up of three former advisers to *The News*. It was to be the board's job to make a decision whenever the faculty adviser and the student editors could not agree on the appropriateness of material for *The St. Albans News*.

That worked fairly well until the famous incident of the cockroach. One day at lunch a Lower School student whose father is nationally prominent found a dead cockroach on his plate. The editors of *The News* wanted to run a front-page story about it. For some reason, the faculty adviser suggested that they should use the Spanish word *cucaracha* instead of cockroach, but he still brought the issue to me. Because of the school's location in Washington, we have many students whose father or mother is nationally prominent. We try hard to avoid either exploiting or embarrassing a student because of who his parents are. It seemed clear to me (and the editors later admitted) that the only reason they wished to run the story was because of the fame of the boy's father. That was so contrary to the way we think young people ought to be treated that I ruled against the story. In response, the editoral board resigned en masse with great cries of censorship. A new editorial board of eleventh graders who had been staffers on *The St. Albans News* was quickly formed, and publication continued throughout the year.

The editors who resigned decided to publish their own newspaper, which they entitled *The Independent*. It a sign of both modern technology (desktop publishing) and our students' knowledge of that technology that this option was open to them. The editors of *The Independent* were able to gain the backing of several alumni who were nationally prominent in the media. I found it interesting that adults would support adolescents against their school without first talking to officials at the school to find out the other side of the story.

The Independent, of course, posed a dilemma for the school. On the one hand, it was somewhat divisive of the student body and since the masthead indicated that it was published by students of St. Albans, an egregious article would certainly have the capability of embarrassing the school. On the other hand, it was an independent operation, and received no support or financial subsidy from the school. The school decided to treat *The Independent* as independent. No attempt was made to control the material printed. Certainly, no threats of retribution were made to any students who participated in *The Independent* and no attempt was made to prevent distribution of *The Indepen-*

dent at St. Albans School except at certain important community events.

After the senior editors graduated, another group of students continued publication of *The Independent* and it continued to be a lively newspaper during the 1989–90 academic year. During the fall of that year, we had much discussion and several meetings about the possibility of merging *The St. Albans News* and *The Independent*. I used to joke that we were providing our students a very important modern skill, that of acquisition and merger negotiations. However, by the spring of 1990, those talks had dwindled off because *The Independent* was not prepared to give up control of what it published.

It seems to me that there are several lessons to be learned from what St. Albans experienced. I had two meetings with the entire editorial board of *The St. Albans News*. My intention was to help the editors understand the particular responsibilities of a school newspaper. What happened was that the leaders of the group felt that they must vigorously defend their position in front of their peers. It is probable that the size of the group made compromise more difficult. A smaller meeting might have had more chance of success.

In fact, we did have a different outcome in another situation. In the spring of 1990, the adviser of the *St. Albans Humor Magazine* brought me its mock-up before it was printed. While we all recognize that a humor magazine may get away with comments that are not appropriate in a newspaper, this edition contained a number of racial remarks and strong sexual innuendoes. All of these were meant as humor, but clearly they would give significant offense to some people. A couple of us on the faculty met with the top two senior editors and were able to work out a satisfactory solution that allowed the *Humor Magazine* to go to print, but removed some of the most offensive material.

This leads to a second lesson that is increasingly becoming apparent to those of us who work with secondary school students. Their idea of what is in good taste, particularly in sexual matters, is quite different from adults' opinions. Most of us who are adults remember telling dirty jokes and making lewd comments among ourselves when we were teenagers, but would never have dared to do it in front of adults. Now young people feel that it is permissible not only to say such things, but to print them. I suspect that the reason for this has been the marked change in what is acceptable on television or in the movies. To use just one example, I recently watched *Back To The Future II,* a comedy aimed at the youth market and rated PG. In the first half hour, teenagers call each other "asshole" and "butthead" and shout "shit." It is hard for some adolescents to understand why such expressions are allowed in movies for general distribution, but are not appropriate in a school newspaper. I have noticed in just the last few years a marked rise in the desire to make public remarks that have sexual innuendoes. Whenever generations have significantly different standards of good taste, there is bound to be tension.

Another lesson is that those of us who believe in the value of schools as communities or families need to do a better job of helping students understand that treatment of individuals which may be acceptable in the national or local press will do great harm in a small community. This is true whether it is criticism of the person or exploiting him because of the name recognition of the boy's parents. With so many students coming from broken or troubled families, it is harder for them to grasp what teachers and administrators mean when they speak of how people in a community or family ought to treat each other.

A fourth lesson about student publications is that the American belief in freedom of the press is so ingrained that people are quick to shout "Censorship!" without thinking through the issue. A number of adults have expressed their belief to me that the school was engaging in censorship. I have usually seen such people reconsider their opinion after I have asked them: "Do you really believe that teenagers who are minors should be allowed to print anything they want? Do you believe that a publication which bears the name St. Albans and which is subsidized by the school should contain sexual innuendoes and one-sided attacks on members of the school family?"

I had been aware that the Supreme Court had made a ruling on high school publications, but at the time we were having our controversy, I did not use that decision as a defense of the school's actions. Whether quoting the Supreme Court would have made any difference, I do not know. What is clear is that the Supreme Court has upheld the right of public school principals to exercise control over student publications. Surely this would be even more true of independent school authorities.

On January 13, 1988, in the case of *Hazelwood School District et al.* v. *Kuhlmeier et al.*, the Supreme Court held:

"(a) First Amendment rights of students in the public schools are not automatically co-extensive with the rights of adults in other settings and must be applied in light of the special characteristics of the school environment. A school need not tolerate student speech that is inconsistent with its basic educational mission, even though the government could not censor similar speech outside the school.

"(b) The school newspaper here cannot be characterized as a forum for public expression. School facilities may be deemed to be public forums only if school authorities have by policy or by practice opened the facilities for indiscriminate use by the general public, or by some segment of the public, such as student organizations. If the facilities have instead been reserved for other intended purposes, communicative or otherwise, then no public forum has been created and school officials may impose reasonable restrictions on the speech of students, teachers, and other members of the school community.

"(c) The standard for determining when a school may punish student expression that happens to occur on school premises is not the standard for determining when a school may refuse to lend its name and resources to the dissimination of student expression. Educators do not offend the First Amendment by exercising editorial control over the style and content of student speech in school-sponsored expressive activities so long as the actions are reasonably related to legitimate pedagological concerns."

Some time later there was a letter to the editor of *The Washington Post* which presented another point of view on the issue. Edwin Fishel wrote:

". . . Although I'm a veteran of seven years of high school and college journalism, I'm in full sympathy with the school authorities' side of the *Hazelwood* case. Why? Because I also had nine years of reporting for daily newspapers whose politics I seldom agreed with. It was a case of working for those publishers or finding some other line of work (a problem that was eventually solved by my draft board).

"I can't imagine a youth more unready for a journalistic career than the scholastic editor who has become used to printing his own views, unsupervised and unrestrained. If he hasn't learned to work for a boss who might overrule him pretty often, he is a spoiled brat whose scholastic training hasn't prepared him for the real world."[1]

There is one other lesson that has also been learned by many people who have tried to control what is printed: such attempts are hazardous and often backfire. In general, the press is interested in stories of censorship. The story about the cockroach appeared in a number of publications around the country and even in Great Britain. My attempt to avoid bringing publicity to a boy because of his father's prominence actually resulted in much more coverage than if the story had just run in *The St. Albans News*. I would have done better to let *The News* carry the story and have that be the end of it.

The issue of freedom of the press and freedom of expression is a very live issue on college campuses today. It has taken a particularly pernicious form when freedom of expression is used to defend racial and religious slurs on minority groups. The colleges are having a difficult time resolving the issue. Our position was that publications which bear the name St. Albans and which are subsidized by the school must represent the values of the school. Those values include compassion and good taste. The two points of view were clearly identified in an article in *The Washington Post,* which quoted me as saying, "Compassion must be part of everything that is done using the name 'St. Albans,' " and quoting one of the editors of *The Independent* as saying, "Compassion should not control what we print."

Off-Campus Behavior

The original problems with *The St. Albans News* in 1988 resulted from its desire to cover the off-campus behavior of students and the school's policy on such behavior. Making judgments about off-campus behavior is a very difficult task for secondary schools.

During the academic year 1987–88 there was a problem because students from a number of independent schools, including St. Albans, were engaging in fighting on weekends. The school sent a letter to all parents indicating that such activity would make a student liable for disciplinary action. It was clear to the parents of the boy who committed the vandalism in the fall of 1988 that the school was going to react through its disciplinary system. Therefore, they withdrew him from St. Albans as soon as they learned of the incident.

In the winter of 1989, three young people not associated with St. Albans were killed in the explosion of a homemade bomb in a garage in Bethesda. The Washington community was shocked and grieved. In the spring of that year television news shows and the press reported that a series of explosions had occurred on a golf course in Bethesda on a Saturday night. No one had been hurt in this particular incident.

About a week later I was visited by legal authorities from Bethesda. They told me they believed eight of our students were involved in these explosions and they were seeking the boys' home phone numbers so they could question them. I supplied the authorities with the home phone numbers and immediately called the parents to tell them that I had done so. Three days later, the school's disciplinary committee met with the boys who had been named. Three admitted that they had constructed and detonated the explosives; five had simply been present and watched during the detonation. The three were expelled from St. Albans and the five were suspended for a short period of time.

There was no question in my mind that the deaths of three youngsters earlier in the year influenced the disciplinary committee on its decision. The committee members believed that if our students could not learn the danger of homemade bombs from the deaths of three other youngsters, they really needed a strong statement from the school. Certainly, the deaths of the other three youngsters contributed to the wide coverage that the press gave to the St. Albans incident. I received several letters from prominent chemists, explaining that they had begun their careers fooling around with homemade explosives and saying that they thought I was too harsh on the students. In general, however, I would say the response of the school family was that in view of the deaths, the expulsions were justified.

However, one concern was voiced fairly frequently. The question was why a boy in the fall, with a prominent father, had been allowed to withdraw while these boys had been expelled. The fact is that at the same meeting when the father first told me that his son had committed the vandalism, he also withdrew his son. Once a boy has withdrawn from the school, there really is no further action for the school to take. Certainly, as the boy began the process of transferring to a boarding school, I was very clear with the boarding school about the details of the incident that led to his withdrawal. In the case of the boys who were expelled for exploding bombs, I had informed their parents of their involvement, rather than the reverse. Three days elapsed and the parents had made no move to withdraw their sons.

The problems of vandalism, off-campus violence, and bombs did produce one very poignant moment for me. After wrestling with the tough decision about what to do with the boys who had set off the bombs, I was walking with the student body as we headed for the chapel. They knew I was going to make some sort of announcement about the incident and the punishment. It really appeared to be the last straw in a difficult year. As we walked along, I suddenly felt a large hand clamped on my shoulder. It was my twelfth grade son who quietly said, "Hang in there, Dad."

One week after graduation that year, I learned that two of our students, a boy who had just finished his junior year and another who had just finished his sophomore year, had been arrested for stealing golf clubs at yet another country club. Again, the disciplinary committee met and both boys were expelled. This incident aroused many questions about the school's response when bad conduct occurs during vacation periods. We wrestled with the dilemma. If the misbehavior occurs on a school night, but off-campus, may it be punished? What about a weekend? What about during spring vacation? What about during the summer?

The other reason the issue is so difficult is that a policy of punishing for off-campus behavior inevitably creates unfairness. The school will be officially aware of some misconduct; it will hear rumors but have no facts about other conduct; and there will be some misconduct of which students are aware but which never comes to the attention of the school authorities. Therefore, the application of any off-campus discipline is uneven, and this is always a source of frustration to young people. However, it seems to me that it would be a very great disservice to our students to let them believe that one kind of behavior is acceptable on campus and another code off-campus. They need to learn that if they belong to a group, their individual behavior will reflect on the group as a whole and may hurt other members of that group. It is interesting to me that more and more schools are taking a stronger position about off-campus behavior. Certainly, that was expressed in the letter by the heads of seven independent schools which I quoted in Chapter Two.

With the publicity that surrounded the issue of freedom of the press and the attention about the golf course bombs, St. Albans was much in the news during the academic year 1988–89. In the summer of that year, an alumnus of the school wrote an article in *Vanity Fair* about St. Albans. Half of the article reflected his own unhappiness with the experience he had at the school in the late '50s and early '60s. The other half talked about the problems of the 1988–89 year. It is hard for me to comment on what happened at St. Albans when the author of the article was a student, but it was very clear to me that in his treatment of the more recent events, he most certainly did not seek balance. He quoted from several people who were critical of the school while the only person he quoted supporting the school was myself. Moreover, he had many of his facts wrong, and repeatedly used innuendo to imply, but not state, an untruth.

The article appeared during summer vacation and when school resumed, I spent our first faculty meeting inviting teachers to ask questions about it. Later I met with each of the high school classes to give students a chance to ask me about the article. The reaction of the students was most interesting. While it is natural, and probably good, that students are critical of those in authority, they also have a strong sense of fair play. Our students knew that the article was not fair, that it inaccurately attacked several of their favorite teachers, and that it did not present a balanced view of the school. I sensed great sympathy for the school's administration in those meetings with students. Perhaps one boy said it best when he rather plaintively asked: "St. Albans students do so many things that are good and are great accomplishments. Why did the article mention none of those?"

Even more interesting has been the reaction to the article in the greater community. Most parents and alumni were sympathetic to the school. In the year following the appearance of the article, annual giving went up, as did applications to the school. Whether there is any connection between those increases and the article itself, I do not know.

Snow

The problems I have already mentioned in this chapter made the 1988–89 school year one of my most difficult ones. It has interested me, however, that neither of these issues have caused as much comment from our alumni as the matter of snow. For many years St. Albans had a policy of never closing because of snow. Even if the public schools or the government itself were closed for snow, St. Albans was open. Generations of boys were taught that getting to school in the snow was a sign of both toughness and the importance of education. It was a source of pride to alumni and students that the school never closed. That pride was less enthusiastically embraced by St. Albans mothers who, after all, had to do most of the driving in the snow.

On the weekend of George Washington's birthday (1979) during my second year as headmaster, Washington was hit with twenty-two inches of snow. We were closed on Monday anyway for the holiday. About 5:00 p.m. on Monday, I received a call from the Bishop who explained that the mayor had called him, asking him to make sure that the Cathedral schools would be closed because any traffic would hamper the snow removal operation. I thought the request a reasonable one. However, because we had not closed before, we did not have a telephone chain. The assistant headmasters and I spent most of Monday evening calling parents to tell them the school would be closed on Tuesday. I was worried, however, that some boy might not get the word. Therefore, about seven o'clock on that snowy morning, I walked the short distance from my house to the school to be sure that any arriving student went home. As I passed the Cathedral, I saw coming toward me my seventy-year-old predecessor who had walked two miles in the snow from his home to take an early service at the Cathedral. Because he had believed passionately in the no-closing policy, my embarrassment was acute and I was tempted to dive into the nearest snowdrift. However, he was, as always, a true gentleman and just greeted me with a cheery "Good morning" as he entered the Cathedral.

On Tuesday evening about five o'clock I again received a phone call at home. This time the caller identified himself as a member of the mayor's staff, and he said, "We want you to close that school again tomorrow." I hit the roof, and shouted into the phone: "The snow has been on the ground for forty-eight hours. Why do you people at city hall always wait until five o'clock to ask us to close the school? That just makes it so hard to contact all our parents. Can't you get yourselves organized and make your request earlier in the day?" Then I heard the laughter in the background. It was a twelfth grader using the telephone in our own drama office to tease the headmaster.

My gullibility about snow did not end then. Several years later Washington was buried under twenty-five inches of snow. After a day in school, the inconvenience to faculty and students trying to get home during the storm was immense. The faculty voted, and I approved, a policy that would link our closing to that of the public schools. Since more and more of our students and faculty now lived so far from the school (many in outer Montgomery County and northern Virginia) and the amount of traffic has increased so dramatically, we needed to change the policy. I heard often from alumni who strongly believed that the school was going soft. I knew that many members of the Governing Board did not approve of the change, and it was to their credit that they allowed the faculty and administration to make this important decision about the operation of the school.

In the spring of 1988, I went on sabbatical and was

living in a Welsh fishing village. The Secretary of the Board, who regularly sent me the minutes of the Board meetings, mailed the third set. I began to read them but did not get through the first paragraph. There, to my horror, were these words: "The Board voted unanimously to rescind the policy about closing on snow days. From henceforth, the school will remain open no matter what weather conditions prevail." I threw the minutes down and said to my wife: "How could they do that behind my back? They wait until I leave the country and then sneak through that change in policy!" All day I grumbled about such an action and went to bed nursing my wounds.

It was not until the next morning that my wife picked up the minutes and read on into the second and third paragraphs. "What is this about the Director of Development saying the blessing and fifteen teachers resigning?" Then I looked more closely at the document and realized that the Secretary had prepared this version of the minutes for my eyes only. Once again, I had fallen victim to snow.

A Boys School

One of the strengths of the American educational system is that, unlike in many other countries, it is decentralized. Even in publicly funded institutions, the federal government has remarkably little power to command. There also exists at the elementary, secondary, and university levels a healthy, totally decentralized, private educational system. What is remarkable, then, is that even without a central authority, once an educational trend gains momentum, it is soon adopted by most parts of the national system. An unfortunate example of this was the way "new math" swept the country in the 1970s. An even clearer example has taken place during the last twenty-five years as hundreds of single-sex institutions have become coeducational. There are only a handful of all-male colleges left in the country, and the number of all-boys schools has been dramatically reduced.

I find two things particularly interesting about this striking change. First, it occurred with almost no empirical evidence to indicate that single-sex education was harmful to students. Educators made the change largely because of assumptions they and the general population held but could not prove. It was clear that sexism existed in our society in pernicious forms. The belief was that by doing away with single-sex educational institutions, we could reduce sexism. What is odd about that assumption is that 90 percent of the population has never been educated in a single-sex institution, and therefore, such institutions can hardly be blamed for general attitudes in society.

The second interesting phenomenon is that those interested in feminism have begun to see that single-sex schools may well be advantageous to girls. There is growing research that this is true. Boys schools, however, appear to remain on the defensive. As Richard Hawley, headmaster of the University School in Ohio, said: "Structuring schools so that they realize what is deepest and truest and best in females is currently regarded as a progressive educational attitude. Structuring schools so that they realize what is deepest and truest and best in males is not currently regarded as a progressive educational attitude (to put it mildly). This is unreasonable."[2]

In the past few years there has been some research about the effects of all-male institutions on academic performance. A study by A. Bryk and V. Lee of seventy-five Catholic high schools showed that students in single-sex schools (male or female) not only did better academically than students in coed schools, but they also exhibited more positive attitudes toward school and better behavior patterns.[3]

An interesting experiment at Hunter College High School in New York (a coeducational institution) was recently conducted with calculus students. Students were randomly distributed into coed, all-boys, and all-girls calculus classes. No one was surprised when the girls did better in the all-girls classes. But they were surprised when the boys in all-boys classes also did better than their counterparts in coed classes.[4]

I believe there are two reasons why academic performance may be higher in single-sex situations. First of all, the opposite sex in a classroom is a distraction. The distraction may be overt with glances, flirting, and conversation. It may be very silent, simply the fear of embarrassing oneself in front of the opposite sex at a time in one's life when one is unsure of how to relate socially. Second, it is very clear that there are gender-specific differences in the physical and mental development of young people. To quote Hawley again:

"Gender-based variations in the tempo and pattern of learning can be identified from the pre-kindergarten through the high school years.

"If the learning styles and learning tempos of boys and girls are at variance, a homogeneous school program—whether curricular or extracurricular—will unavoidably miss either the masculine or feminine mark, if not both."[5]

An interesting article in *Time* magazine (May 21, 1990) suggested there is evidence that "putting elementary school black boys in separate classrooms, without girls or whites, under the tutelage of black, male teachers" may significantly improve their school performance. Of course, such an idea flies in the face of twenty-five years of civil rights activity, but it does suggest that educating boys in an all-male environment may be beneficial.

An even more important question for gender education than academic progress is personal growth. There has never been any research indicating that graduates of good boys schools are in any way stunted in their personal growth. There are two reasons why single-sex schools may, in fact, be good for boys. The development of a strong identity is essential for any young person. Self-definition occurs partly by association with those similar to oneself. The bonding that goes on in a single-sex situation may well be stronger than in a mixed-gender atmosphere. Certainly loyalty to one's childhood friends and to educational institutions has traditionally been very strong among the graduates of single-sex institutions.

The second reason is even more compelling. Fifty percent of all American youngsters live in a single-parent household at some time in their lives before they graduate from high school. Eighty percent of those households are headed by women. Even boys who live with both parents throughout their youth often have fathers who lead exceedingly busy lives with little time to spend with their sons. In modern America, few sons have an opportunity to work alongside their fathers, as they did in an agricultural society. Moreover, the extended family of uncles and grandfathers frequently does not live in the same town as the young person.

For all these reasons, male role models who are not fathers or relatives are terribly important in the growth of identity in young men. While boys schools today see the advantages of hiring women faculty members, it is still true that the percentage of men on the faculty at a boys school is usually higher than at a coed school. These men spend many hours with students and provide important role models for them. I was fascinated recently to hear the principal of a Russian school complain that there were not enough men on the faculty at her school. She said she felt that the boys needed more men as examples.

The reasons I have cited above as strengths of boys schools do not indicate that every boy should go to an all-male institution. But I do believe they suggest that for some boys, single-sex education can be very beneficial. What is good is that parents and students have a choice at the elementary and secondary level. The pluralism of American society which allows choice is one of the greatest strengths of our country. I think it is unfortunate that market pressures have now meant that for young men there is virtually no choice for collegiate education. If they want to go to college, they go to a coeducational institution. I believe it is healthy for our country and for some young men that before college, the choice of all-male education is still available.

It is clear that two sexes are part of the natural order. Gender differences are not something imposed by a misguided society; they are at the very core of life on this planet. As long as that is true, it is reasonable to suppose that schools which aim to serve a particular gender may be of value to many young people.

Any discussion of gender-based education reminds me of the man who had been raised in very humble circumstances and then became quite a success in life. He went to the head of an independent school and said: "I was disadvantaged. I don't want my son to be. I'd like to enroll him in your school."

The head of the school replied: "I'm terribly sorry. There must be some misunderstanding here. This is an all-girls school."

The man said: "Exactly. I want my son to have every opportunity I missed."

The Church School

As society has become more secular, educators in the independent sector have tended to respond in one of two ways. The last quarter-century has seen a significant rise in the number of fundamentalist and evangelical schools. These hold a narrow view of the sources of truth and often impose a strict, personal morality. They appeal to a growing but particular group of Americans. On the other hand, many traditional independent schools have moved away from their founding religious principles to appeal to more diverse and broader segments of our society. In the process, they have often watered down the message their founders wished to impart. Spiritual and moral values are still discussed, but much less is heard of God or religious commitment. The word "Christian" may be used as a well-meaning adjective, but the word "Christ" is rarely heard except as an example of a good man. Nonetheless, there are a number of schools that have chosen to seek a balance of remaining a true church school while appealing to students from a wide variety of religious backgrounds and traditions. This is a difficult task, but living in a state of tension is part of life in the twentieth century.

St. Albans School is committed to the undertaking. We are, of course, a Cathedral school, but much more than that, we believe there are benefits derived from being a church school.

There is no doubt that religion has played a major role in shaping Western civilization. Art, music, architecture, literature, and politics have been greatly influenced by the Old and New Testaments and the religions that derived from them. Yet, because of our belief in the separation of church and state, public schools can do little to help students know and understand these forces. In an interesting reversal, Russian priests are now allowed to teach in Soviet schools after the regular school day. It is even possible that within the next five years, religion will be part of the regular curriculum in Soviet schools. How ironic that will be since it is illegal to teach religion in American public schools.

The teaching of religion was not so important in a day when most young people in America belonged to some sort of religious congregation and attended services regularly. As our society has become increasingly secular, even those who say they are believers are less inclined to be regular churchgoers. Many young people are growing up illiterate about religion. The most obvious example is that so many young people are almost totally ignorant of the teachings of the Bible. In a church school the Bible can be studied academically so that its stories, histories, and view of the human condition become part of the intellectual base for students. Chapel services also add to the musical heritage of students. I suspect that very few high school students other than those in church schools are exposed at school to regular doses of Bach, Pachelbel, and Vaughan Williams.

In Chapter Six I wrote of moral education. While it is clearly possible to be a highly moral person without any religious beliefs, I find that it is easier for a chuch school to take and hold a moral position. Without a theological foundation, each moral decision becomes subject to debate and ultimately the person who makes the decision has no established authority to fall back on. I think it was easier for St. Albans to take an early stand on AIDS because of the strength the school derived from the church. This was also demonstrated in the controversy with *The St. Albans News*. A student might say that compassion was much less important than the truth. A church school must hold them both as high values and can insist on compassion being part of anything that is done in the name of the school. To quote again the Supreme Court in the Hazelwood decision: "A school need not tolerate student speech that is inconsistent with its basic educational mission, even though the government could not censor similar speech outside the school." If that basic educational mission is grounded in the biblical view of human relationships, then the school can insist on biblical values. I have had a number of people who are applying to St. Albans School say to me: "Even though I am not a Christian, I would rather have my son in a school that stands for something and comes from a particular tradition than in a school without any religious heritage."

For example, the word "love" is used with a great many different meanings in our society. Someone who has read of the biblical view of God's love toward mankind knows that it is a love that is both deep and caring, but also extremely demanding. God does set standards for human beings and He is grieved when they do not meet those standards. In the same way, there are some people who think that for a school to be loving, it has to accept almost any misbehavior or lack of performance from a student. On the other hand, a school with a theological view recognizes that to be loving is to ask for the best that is within someone. "Tough love" is a phrase that is applicable to theological discussions and to a strong school.

Simply by being at chapel, by hearing the words of the prayers and the Bible and the speakers, something must become ingrained in the minds of students. Even if we, who speak in chapel, totally fail, the repetition of the great words of the Prayer Book reinforces a view of human nature and human relationships that I believe is important for our students to make part of their own consciousness. Think of the words they will hear: "We have erred and strayed like lost sheep. We have left undone those things which we ought to have done, and we have done those things which we ought not to have done." Or "You see your children growing up in an unsteady and confusing world. Help them to take failure not as a measure of their worth, but as a chance for a new start." Or "Oh God, who has taught us that in quietness and confidence shall be our strength. Oh God, make us instruments of your peace." And perhaps most profoundly, "Almighty God, without Thee we are not able to please Thee."

This is one of the reasons why the first word that would come to the minds of my students, if they were asked about chapel services, would be "repetition." They believe they like change and the new. And yet human beings do have a need for ritual and repetition.

My favorite minor example is seating in a classroom. Most teachers find that if they do not assign seats in a classroom, within the first day or two most students will stake out a particular seat or section of the room in which they sit and in which they continue to sit throughout the semester. Some even become highly indignant if a free spirit tries to take what they consider "their" seat.

To use another example, while the excitement of athletics is one of its major appeals, it is also true that sports in America are highly ritualized. Football has its marching bands, cheerleaders, and solemn moment of the toss of a coin. No one needs to tell a baseball fan to take a seventh inning stretch, yet they all do it.

The ritual of chapel services is often considered frustrating or boring by students, but I find it frequently mentioned by alumni as something they value now as they look back on their school days. I remember at a recent gathering of a twenty-fifth class reunion, one alumnus said: "I have recently been separated from my wife and children and over the last few years I have had some ups and downs in business. The sense of stability and permanence that I got at St. Albans has helped sustain me."

While the ritual exerts a very subtle influence in regular chapel, in moments of great tragedy that ritual can be of particular importance. St. Albans alumni still remember being taken into the chapel to be told of the death of President Kennedy. When I had to tell our students that one of their favorite teachers had AIDS, I did it in a regular chapel service. The fact that my sad announcement could be followed by prayers and organ music, and that those who wanted to do so felt free to stay behind to pray or weep, made the experience less embarrassing and more meaningful than if it had been a special assembly in a theater or gymnasium.

In the spring of 1989 a fourth grader was in an automobile accident. He lingered in a coma for four or five days and then died. His sixteen-year-old sister had been driving the car and she was known to many of our students. Thus, Lower and Upper School students were all affected by the tragedy. I had a parent call me and say: "Well, at a good school when something like this happens, they immediately bring in grief counselors to help the students get through the crisis."

I replied: "If there is any individual student who is having a particular problem, we will certainly get him counseling. But as a school, we are going to respond like a Cathedral school. We will cry because we have lost a friend; we will go to church; we will give thanks that we had the opportunity to know this young man and we will commend him into the hands of the God who loves him more than we do. And then we'll get on with our lives, because that's the way Christians handle death." A church school has both the opportunity and the responsibility to handle such situations in that manner.

Being a church school also serves our students long after they have graduated. Many of our alumni return to the chapel to be married or have their children baptized. Our chapel is the scene of a fair number of funerals and memorial services for alumni or past parents. To return to the school, the scene of their youth, for important milestones in their family and personal lives not only strengthens the feelings alumni have for the school, but also gives them a sense of permanence or what my predecessor, Charles Martin, described as a "bedrock constancy."

Some of the benefits of a church school I have mentioned already may have appeal to nonbelievers. But for those of us who are believers, the church school has yet another and more important aspect. Egocentricity is a natural characteristic of human beings, and it is perhaps at its most predominant among adolescents. A good and effective church school constantly points students beyond themselves, beyond even human concerns, to something more important, more lasting. The church school teaches that man is not the measure of all things. It points beyond men and women toward the God who created them and loved them, and who reveals Himself most fully in the person of Christ.

Once in a while, a student comes into my office and says: "Mr. Mullin, why do I have to go to chapel? I don't get anything out of it."

And I say to him: "Young man, we do not have a chapel so you can get something out of it. It does not exist for your benefit. We have a chapel for God's benefit. He wants and needs us to worship Him." Inevitably, the student leaves my office shaking his head as if saying to himself, "I always thought the guy was crazy. Now I know it." But I like to think that years later he may come to understand what I meant.

I cannot close a discussion of the church school without telling my favorite chapel story. Early in my time at St. Albans, I was baptizing a fourth grader. The baptismal font in our chapel was given to the school in memory of a St. Albans father and is a piece of rough-hewn Maine granite. I knew the fourth grader spent his summers in Maine. During the baptism I was preaching a sermon on the boy's life at school, his life in Maine, his new life in Christ all coming together in this particular baptismal font at the school. Just as I was reaching the conclusion, the fourth grader looked up at me and said: "Don't you know it's illegal to take granite out of Maine?"

Pressure

In April 1990, I attended the second meeting of a group of boys schools. There were nine headmasters there, representing leading schools in New England, the mid-Atlantic area, the Midwest, and Texas. At one point in our discussions, we talked about admissions and what we could learn from people whose sons we had admitted but who chose to send their sons to another school. None of the headmasters said they felt they were losing many students to coed schools. At least half of them said there was one common theme when they lost someone they had admitted. Over and over again, they were hearing from parents: "You have an excellent school, but it is too demanding. There is too much pressure. I can send my son to another school which is less demanding, and he will have just as good a chance of getting into college."

I was fascinated to learn that across the country, people who were willing to spend considerable amounts of money to give their sons an independent school education were looking for one that was not too demanding. That had been a matter of concern at St. Albans School during the 1988-89 school year. The Governing Board appointed a long-range planning committee, made up of alumni, parents, and teachers, to look at the needs of the school in the years ahead. One of the issues that emerged was a division of opinion between those who thought that we were putting too much pressure on young people and those who thought that such attitudes explained why America is slipping behind certain other parts of the world.

Recently I heard of a poll that asked Americans: "What are the most important qualities of a parent?" The five qualities most frequently named were patience, understanding, love, kindness, and honesty. All of us who have been parents or teachers know that it is difficult to practice these qualities at all times, yet we try to incorporate them in our relationships with young people.

What is most striking about the list is not the attributes it contains but the ones that are missing. There is no mention of discipline or the establishment of standards. There is no expectation that parents will bring out the best that is within their children, or help them grow into accomplished and talented adults. Tough love seems an unknown concept. Parenting is seen as warm and cuddly.

Usually such attitudes are defended on the grounds that children need acceptance. Their fear is that anything that is demanding might damage a child's self-esteem. Setting high standards creates the possibility that they will not be met, possibly hurting a child's sense of self-worth. By teaching children that whatever they manage to accomplish is acceptable, parents try to ensure that their children will never suffer or come to doubt themselves.

I hear from an increasing number of people in school work that this attitude toward parenting is also expected of teachers. Parents want their children to feel good about themselves and about school. If teachers make demands for excellence, children will feel pressure, and if a child does not respond to high expectations, his self-image may be diminished. Success without stress is the goal.

The problem with these attitudes is that they ignore two important facts of human nature. First, we must recognize that self-worth comes from accomplishment. To work hard, to meet high demands, and then to succeed are the ingredients for developing self-confidence. We all know that our greatest satisfactions come when we have had to struggle and overcome obstacles. But for some reason, we often want our children to have an easier time and to spared from making the effort.

The second fact is that disappointment, frustration, and even failure come to all human beings from time to time and only by learning to deal with minor setbacks can we be prepared to face more important disappointments. Yet because we love our children, and do not like to see them in pain, we try to protect them from disappointment and discouragement. One way of doing this is by making sure that demands put on them will never exceed their grasp. Obviously, too much discouragement and failure can make a young person give up and have a permanent sense of inferiority. But never to experience frustration or difficult challenges will leave a person without the strength to handle later problems.

Many people have recognized that athletics and other extracurricular activities provide the sort of structure that leads to growth. These have the potential for success and failure, disappointment and joy. They prepare young people for life. But sometimes we think that academic work should be different. We want students to feel good about it. In our concern for self-image, we worry about the effects of demanding hard work and true commitment to excellence. Much of the decline in academic standards in this country has come from the "feel good" theory of education. But in the long run it does more harm to students because it leaves them unprepared for the demands of life.

If this is true in the academic life of young people, it appears to be even more so in their moral life. We as adults appear unprepared to set high moral standards for our children. We tell them that one should not make moral judgments because we must be willing to accept a variety of lifestyles. We allow them to think that success, dishonestly or unfairly earned, carries the same rewards as success that has been truly accomplished. Our society appears to have failed to give young people the message that true self-esteem cannot be attained by either antisocial behavior or self-indulgence.

The task for both teachers and parents is to provide young people with the warmth, the support, and the caring that they need while also helping them to grow, to stretch, and to learn to meet both disappointment and high standards.

The School Community

When I talk with alumni about their experiences at St. Albans, they, of course, mention the academic preparation they received as being important in later life. But almost all of them try to describe something else they valued about their secondary school experience. Often they speak of the friends they made who have remained with them throughout their lives. Some use a word such as "community." Those who have listened to various headmasters may use the phrase "school family." The more modern may even speak of "bonding." Whatever terms are used to describe it, the experience of being part of a group, sharing both challenges and successes with other young people and feeling that they have belonged to something bigger than themselves, something good, something permanent, is a very important one to most alumni. It is one of the reasons they like to come back to reunions and other alumni functions. It is significant that even a teacher at a large public high school such as Patrick Welsh can say: "In the future, good schools will, I think, resemble good families in their caring qualities."[6]

Alumni also worry that the school of today has lost

some of this important quality. They ask the question, "When today's students are having their twenty-fifth reunion, will they also speak of the community or the school family?" There are several reasons why these concerns of alumni are very valid. A typical graduating class today is 40 percent larger than those of twenty-five years ago. The smaller the group, the easier it is to maintain a sense of family. The school has worked hard to increase the racial, economic, and international diversity of its student body. Obviously, the more heterogenous the group is when it first comes together, the harder it is to create a community. The school has also significantly broadened its offerings in both academics and extracurricular activities. While this makes for more choice and a much richer experience, it also means that two classmates may have fewer experiences in common. Finally, the deterioration of the American family, and the reduced likelihood of a youngster experiencing a sense of community within his residential neighborhood, mean that the idea of community or family is less real to our students. It is ironic that just at a time when young people are more likely to need the school to provide a sense of togetherness, other factors make it harder for the school to do so.

There are a number of ways a school can build a sense of community. Perhaps the most important is that the leaders of the school and the teachers have it as a goal, articulate this priority, and base decisions on it. At St. Albans we believe that coming together once a day in one room for a shared family-style meal in which students from different classes and faculty members sit at assigned tables is a terribly important community-building experience. We also find that coming together in chapel and having a curriculum that is not a wide-open smorgasbord adds to the shared experience of a St. Albans education. The challenge for educators who believe in the concept of the school as a community or a family is to provide a range of experiences—academic and extracurricular—that meet the needs of individual students and still create enough shared experiences that students do, indeed, learn what it is to live in community.

It is also important for young people to learn that communities do not exist in just one moment of time. The young are naturally egocentric about time. Anything that happened more than eighteen years ago is ancient history. The Battle of Verdun and the Tet Offensive were almost contemporary with each other. Of course, schools such as St. Albans encourage alumni involvement because they are very dependent on alumni for financial support. They also welcome alumni back because it is a service to former students to keep them in touch with their youth and the friends of their childhood. Schools should also maintain alumni activities because of the message it sends to present students. It is the message that a school, like any community, does not exist just in the present. It is indeed a community of those who have come before us, those who are here now, and those who will follow after us.

Captain Frederick Hauck, who commanded the Space Shuttle *Discovery* on the first flight after the *Challenger* disaster, carried with him on an earlier flight a small painting of Saint Alban. That painting is now on display in the Common Room of the school. I am fond of saying that a school which values traditions yet prepares boys for the future is named after a third-century saint who has traveled in a space shuttle. It is this idea of an ongoing community that we wish all our graduates to carry with them.

Chapter Eight

Generations Yet To Come

At the end of my thirteenth year as headmaster, I attended a party being held by a St. Albans class which was celebrating its twentieth reunion. One member of the class, who also serves on the Governing Board of the school, introduced me to his classmates as "the new headmaster." To those at the reunion, he was absolutely right. My predecessor had been at the school for twenty-seven years. While he and I have served a school that values traditions, we have both known that a headmaster must look toward what lies ahead. In this final chapter I want to do just that—first, to what I consider the greatest threat to our schools, then to what I believe to be the ten most important challenges for the 1990s.

Every time I mention one particular issue to headmasters of other independent schools, I know I have touched a nerve. That issue is the increasing interference with the educational process by legal concerns and constraints. The problem is twofold. First, the American propensity for lawsuits has driven insurance rates to the point where they are a serious financial drain on schools and even threaten the existence of some valuable programs within schools. For example, when eight students were killed on Mount Hood, shock waves rippled through the insurance industry, and there was a real danger that insurance for any outdoor programs would become prohibitively expensive. The number of suits resulting from sports injuries, even when parents knowingly allow their children to participate in contact sports, has put a very heavy insurance burden on both the manufacturers of equipment and schools that offer such sports.

The possibility of a time-consuming and expensive lawsuit faces any school administrator whenever he thinks of applying major discipline to a student or getting rid of an ineffective teacher. School heads face a public which in the abstract calls for greater discipline and a higher quality of teaching, yet which often supports an individual who challenges a school's decision in court. The problem for the school administrator is not so much that he may lose a case; one would hope that he would try always to act in such a way that his decisions have a good chance of being supported by the courts. But even if the lawsuit is won, vast amounts of time and unrecoverable financial resources of the school will be used to prove innocence.

Second, an increasing number of legal and administrative rules curtail the freedom of schools to pursue what is educationally best for the students. For example, when one or two teachers out of all the thousands of teachers in Pennsylvania were guilty of child molestation, the legislature passed a law requiring that any new teacher being hired must be investigated by the state police. Child molestation is a horrible crime with lasting damage and one can understand how a member of the legislature does not want to face the next election and have his opponent point the finger, saying "The incumbent refused to protect our children." But to impose a bureaucratic nightmare of state police checks on every new teacher drastically hampers those schools that must make quick replacements when they lose a teacher. One must wonder whether such a system provides any real protection.

Every headmaster I know has a stock group of favorite tales of frivolous lawsuits and absurd regulations. Every headmaster I know perceives that the problem has gotten significantly worse, and looks for even more problems in the 1990s. A major issue for all Americans is how much we want our schools run by educators, and how much we want them run by the courts. A major issue for every school is how it can protect itself in the legal arena and still provide the quality of education it feels its students deserve.

Ten Challenges

What follows is my list of ten challenges facing schools in the 1990s. First, there will be a continued financial challenge. Where can schools find the resources to provide teachers with a living wage, much less one that is competitive with other professions? I know of young people in their first year out of law school who earn more money than any teacher in my school. I know of legal secretaries without a college education who earn more than the median teacher at my school. Teachers may not expect to earn as much as lawyers, but if they are to stay in teaching, they must have a wage that permits them a decent lifestyle and the opportunity to have a family. If they are to be dedicated and effective teachers, they must have this income without having to moonlight at other jobs.

The second challenge I see for secondary schools is to prepare students for the rapid expansion of information that will occur throughout their lifetimes. As the sum total of human knowledge doubles in less than two years, they must be prepared to handle ever-increasing amounts of new material. This will mean that they must be trained to be lifetime learners, and regard formal schooling as only

Ten Challenges

1. There will be a continued financial challenge.
2. We must prepare students for the rapid expansion of information that will occur throughout their lifetime.
3. The third challenge is to use the new technology to enhance education and to make sure that students are familiar with it.
4. Preparation for this world—continually shrinking—must be an important part of secondary education.
5. We must give students an opportunity to work with and understand young people from other backgrounds and cultures.
6. The sixth challenge is to help students prepare for a world in which they will have to make so many more choices than their ancestors did.
7. The schools must find ways to use constructively the energy, expertise, and concerns of parents. Schools must also provide the environment and support systems that will be useful to students in a world in which family life has so disintegrated.
8. The schools must provide a demanding enough curriculum to meet the needs of the most talented students while bringing along those others who, at this time in their lives, are not ready to move at such a pace but will be ready to handle university work.
9. The ninth challenge is to allow students to develop expertise in certain areas and yet give them the breadth of experience and the sense of community they need at this age.
10. The most important challenge: Help students grow into men and women of moral discernment and strength.

the first step in an ongoing process of education. Moreover, it will be very important that they be trained in the skill of shifting rapidly though vast amounts of material and picking out what is most essential for the task at hand.

The expansion of knowledge presents a challenging paradox for educators. On the one hand, the information explosion requires emphasis on method. It appears very important that students learn how to handle vast amounts of information. On the other hand, the sheer volume of knowledge creates a need for certain shared information to facilitate communication. Hirsch's point that cultural literacy is essential because one cannot take time to explain every term or expression one uses is even more valid as we are inundated with ever more and more facts. Diane Ravitch, author of *What Do Our Seventeen-Year-Olds Know?,* made this point in an article about the 1988 election:

"The Presidential candidates have been roundly criticized for failing to discuss the issues, and they probably deserve it. But if there is anything to be said in explanation of their behavior, it is this: that even if the candidates were discussing the real issues, the American public doesn't seem to know enough about them to follow a serious debate. How can the candidates debate American policy in Nicaragua and El Salvador when the public doesn't know where they are and which side we are on? How can they debate the contemporary relevance of the Monroe Doctrine when the phrase is meaningless to many? What does it mean for George Bush to accuse Michael Dukakis of being a New Deal Democrat when many people have no idea what the New Deal was? How persuasive is the charge by Dukakis that Bush is guilty of McCarthyism when large numbers don't know that the term means, or think that Senator

Joseph McCarthy was famous for opposing the war in Vietnam?"[1]

The third challenge is to use the new technology to enhance education and to make sure that students are familiar with it. Every student planning to attend a university should be computer literate. I would argue that even students not bound for university should have some familiarity with computers. It may make the difference in their ability to find a job. Because it can be so useful in improving the quality of writing, the word processor ought to be introduced to all students. I am always impressed when I see English or history teachers taking extra time to sit down on a one-to-one basis with a student and go over papers line by line to improve the quality of writing. How much more effective that would be if, instead of bringing in a paper, the student brought in a disk and teacher and student worked together on a word processor to learn how to edit and improve the student's writing. Of course, putting new technology in the hands of all students will require a major capital outlay, one that will undoubtedly strain any school. But it should be a goal toward which schools are working if they are to prepare the children of the moon for the twenty-first century.

All of us are aware of our continually shrinking world. I have written much about it in earlier chapters. Without question, preparation for this world must be an important part of secondary education in the 1990s. The Stanford plan is worth considering, not as a model to be followed by all secondary schools, but as a stimulus for discussion and a challenge for our thinking. As was reported in the press during the mid-to-late 1980s, Stanford University went through a long internal process of considering cultural literacy and cultural diversity in its curricula. It developed a new plan whereby undergraduates will have some choice about what courses they take in what used to be called Western civilization. The curriculum and reading list will be arranged so that no matter which electives are chosen, every student is exposed to the same six books or authors. This is done not only because these works are considered so important in the Western cultural tradition, but so that there can be a common intellectual experience for all Stanford undergraduates. This, of course, is designed to encourage dialogue outside of the classroom. The six books or authors are the Bible, Plato, a Greek tragedy (which changes each year—in 1988 it was Antigone), Machiavelli, Rousseau, and Marx. Moreover, each course must look not only at Western civilization, but also at material that draws substantially from another tradition. Stanford describes this as a work that will provide a friction with traditional Western culture. The hope here is to expose students to something from the non-Western world and also to have them look at Western culture from an outside perspective. It is possible to understand something by studying it carefully and by studying it in comparison with a very different universe.

One of the ways of helping students to prepare for an ever-shrinking world is to provide them with a more diverse experience within their own school. This is the fifth challenge I would put before schools: to give students an opportunity to work with and understand young people from other backgrounds and cultures because this will help them to adjust to new situations when they are adults. Because they can decide whom to admit and to reject, independent schools have greater opportunities and greater challenges to build a diverse student body. It is a difficult task, but there are few schools that can be complacent that they are doing the task successfully. All schools, public and independent, can develop exchange programs which help bring students from other cultures into their midst and give their students exposure to new worlds.

The diversity issue is not just one of the makeup of the student body, however. It also deals with what is taught as people from a variety of cultures enter the mainstream of American education. They are asking more and more that their own cultural experience be included in the curriculum. How to do that while still providing all students with the cultural literacy to function in the United States is an increasingly important challenge.

The sixth challenge is to help students prepare themselves for a world in which they will have to make so many more choices than their ancestors did. Not only does the range of career opportunities open to college students increase each year, but more and more adults are now feeling that it is appropriate to make choices about career changes even in mid-life or later. The traditional pattern of courtship followed by permanent marriage has been replaced by a whole range of lifestyles. There is almost no stigma today for couples to live together without being married or to divorce. Homosexuality carries a continuing stigma, but changes in laws and administrative rules are reducing that. Today only a minority of Americans live in the traditional family pattern of man, woman, and children in the same house.

There is much greater freedom of choice about where one lives, how one spends leisure time, and even how much one chooses to work. I believe our society is offering more choices about style, whether it be styles in dress or speech patterns or appearance. In the educational reforms of the 1960s, schools tried to prepare students to make choices by giving them many more choices. This is one way to help people in decision-making. However, most educators today are worried about giving students choices for which they are not prepared or which might have long-term detrimental consequences. As schools moved away from the mode of the 1960s into more traditional patterns, they did not escape the need to prepare students for a world of great choice.

I believe that parent consumerism will continue to increase during the 1990s, and this is the seventh challenge for schools. I have spoken of parents at some length. The challenge is twofold. The schools must find ways to use constructively the energy, expertise, and concerns of parents. Schools must also provide the environment and support systems that will be useful to students in a world in which family life has so disintegrated.

An eighth challenge for most schools is to handle the range of students which make up the student body. Leading independent schools could fill their ranks with nothing but topflight scholars, and other schools could sift out such youngsters so that they really have a separate school experience. I believe that either course would be a very limiting and unwise one. The challenge is to provide a demanding enough curriculum to meet the needs of the most talented students while bringing along those others who, at this time in their lives, are not ready to move at such a pace but will be ready to handle university work. The challenge becomes even more difficult if one believes, as I do, that these two groups of students not only should interact socially and in extracurricular activities, but should have as much academic interaction as possible. If the challenge is met well, both the top students and the average gain from academic interaction with each other.

The ninth challenge is one that became harder to accomplish in the 1980s. We live in an increasingly specialized world. Moreover, the colleges appear to be sending the message that they are looking for students with expertise and enthusiasm in particular areas and who will bring something interesting and unique to the campus. Students have responded by pursuing particular interests and skills to the exclusion of others. This has meant that their interests have become narrower just at an age when their vision ought to be broadening. Moreover, it means that schools are becoming collections of specialists and the sense of community may be significantly hampered. I believe that in a world of great change, where even the family is not stable, belonging to a strong community is a terribly important experience for adolescents. To allow students to develop expertise in particular areas and yet give them the breadth of experience and the sense of community they so need at this age is a difficult challenge for educators.

Finally, I believe that the most important challenge is helping students grow into men and women of moral discernment and strength. We know that no matter what skills or knowledge or competencies they acquire, if they do not have ethical vision and ethical courage, they will not improve the world. In Chapter Six I suggested a few ways that schools might try to instill essential values in students.

Those schools that have a religious heritage can approach moral questions from a particular tradition; however, as all schools have become more diverse, the question of values has become much more difficult. Students from different backgrounds arrive with different assumptions and experiences and we are more hesitant about imposing our own values on others. Most of us believe in such abstractions as compassion, integrity, and respect for the rights of others. However, when it comes time to put such terms into practice or when they come into conflict with other values such as success, material well-being, and self-esteem, we find a myriad of interpretations and expectations.

I believe that young people best understand values and develop moral strength when they think of ethics as statements about what strengthens and what destroys personal relationships. For today's students, rules imposed from outside carry little validity. So many rule-makers are vague and uncertain themselves, and those who appear to be sure are often dogmatic. Students do understand and value relationships. They can appreciate that certain actions will strengthen and that others will harm them. Frequently, even the Ten Commandments are presented as abstract principles. In fact, they were designed as a personal response to a particular act by God for the purpose of enhancing Israel's relationship with Him and improving relationships of the people of Israel with each other. In Exodus, the Ten Commandments are not introduced with an abstraction but with a personal statement: "I am the Lord your God who brought you up out of the land of Egypt. You should have no other gods but me."[2]

We can help students to understand that the reason integrity is at the heart of ethics is because a lack of integrity is so destructive to human relationships. It may be difficult for them to grasp, but they can be helped to see that their sexual behavior affects not only their present relationships but also their future ones. And certainly how one treats other people in all one's interactions has both an immediate and long-range effect on one's relationships.

In both Judaism and Christianity the highest ethical behavior has always been seen as the response to a personal relationship with God. In the secular world, emphasis on relationships can help a student think through more deeply the consequences of his or her actions. Most of us respond more to personal situations than we do to abstractions. Emphasis on relationships can thus help students do what they know is right.

A Last Word

The children of the moon are in some ways unique in human development. They were born after man first broke the bonds of earth and they will become adults just as we move into the twenty-first century, with all the promise and dangers it has. Because of the pace of change, the world they inherit will be significantly different from any that other generations have known. They will have new opportunities and new challenges, and they will use a new vocabulary to describe their world and themselves. But it is also true that in the face of that newness, they will have the same human desires and anxieties, the same frustrations and joys, that men and women have always had. Like instruction in the past, the education of the children of the moon has the potential not only to prepare them for a new world, but to make it a brave and better new world.

I close with the words of the late David Aloian. He typifies both education's potential to affect change and its enduring appeal. David's father was an Armenian immigrant. After coming to America he spent his life as a factory worker in an aluminum plant in upstate New York. He sent to Europe for a mail-order bride. Their son entered Harvard at sixteen, was later Headmaster of Concord Academy and then Belmont HIll School. David explained why he chose education for his life's work:

"Perhaps as the oldest child of poor immigrant parents, one who was so disadvantaged that he could neither read, write, nor speak a word of English at the time he entered public school kindergarten in that unpromising year 1933, I was bound to become too zealous a believer in what school could accomplish. After all, if school could take a person from one language and culture to another, from European peasantry to Harvard College in sixteen years, it must be the single most powerful transforming, life-changing, perhaps world-changing agency. Oh, I was aware of several other life-changing agencies—my family, the church, the national culture—but next to school they seemed relatively powerless. So I believed with all the certain ardor of youth and became a teacher."[3]

Notes

Chapter One

1. National Commission on Excellence in Education, *A Nation at Risk* (Washington, D.C.: U.S. Department of Education, 1983).

2. Arthur G. Powell, Eleanor Farrar, and David K. Cohen, *The Shopping Mall High School* (Boston: Houghton-Mifflin, 1985).

3. E. D. Hirsch, Jr., *Cultural Literacy* (Boston: Houghton-Mifflin, 1987).

4. Allan Bloom, *The Closing of the American Mind* (New York: Simon and Schuster, 1987).

5. Michael Collins, *Carrying the Fire* (New York: Farrar, Strauss, and Giroux, 1974), 469–71.

6. Collins, 471.

7. *The Book of Common Prayer* (New York: Seabury Press, 1979), 370. The titles of Chapters Two through Eight come from *The Book of Common Prayer*.

Chapter Two

1. Allan Bloom, *The Closing of the American Mind* (New York: Simon and Schuster, 1987).

2. Patricia Marks Greenfield, *Harvard Education Letter,* March 1990 (Cambridge: Harvard University Press, 1990).
3. Greenfield.
4. Greenfield.
5. Kenneth J. Cooper, "Campus Life Reportedly Deteriorating," *The Washington Post,* April 30, 1990.
6. Jacob H. Montwieler, "A Brother at The Wall," *St. Albans Bulletin* (Washington, D.C.: St. Albans School, Summer 1990), 12.

Chapter Three

1. Allan Bloom, *The Closing of the American Mind* (New York: Simon and Schuster, 1987).
2. National Commission of Excellence in Education, *A Nation at Risk* (Washington, D.C.: U.S. Department of Education, 1983), 11.
3. Andree Aelion Brooks, *Children of Fast Track Parents* (New York: Viking, 1989), 29.
4. Brooks, 29.
5. Brooks, 31.
6. Brooks, 16.
7. Brooks, 133.
8. Patrick Welsh, *Tales Out of School* (New York: Penguin Books, 1986), 41.
9. Brooks, 144.
10. Welsh, 43.
11. Brooks, 208.
12. John Silber, *Straight Shooting* (New York: Harper and Row, 1989), xiv.
13. Craig Bowman, "Adults Must Say 'No'—To Save Children," *Education Week,* February 24, 1988.
14. Midge Decter, *Liberal Parents, Radical Children* (New York: Coward, McCann, and Geoghegan, 1975), 36–37.

Chapter Four

1. John Naisbitt, *Megatrends* (New York: Warner Books, 1984).

2. *Time,* May 23, 1988.
3. Naisbitt, 260.
4. Naisbitt, 261.
5. Naisbitt, 261.
6. Robert Townsend, *Further Up the Organization* (New York: Alfred A. Knopf, 1984), 243.

Chapter Five

1. Allan Bloom, *The Closing of the American Mind* (New York: Simon and Schuster, 1987).
2. E. D. Hirsch, Jr., *Cultural Literacy* (Boston: Houghton-Mifflin, 1987).
3. William J. Bennett, *James Madison High School* (Washington, D.C.: U.S. Department of Education, 1987).
4. Ernest L. Boyer and Terrel H. Bell, "Already a Quarter of Our Workers Use Computers in Their Jobs, and the Trend Is Increasing," in "Education," *American Agenda* (Camp Hill, Pa.: Book of the Month Club, 1988), 170.
5. *Yale College Program of Studies,* 1987–88, 16–17.
6. *The Underachieving Curriculum: Assessing U.S. School Mathematics from an International Perspective* (Champaign, Ill.: Stipes, 1987), vii.
7. Donald J. Brown, *Report on the Mathematics Program of St. Albans School* (Washington, D.C.: St. Albans School, 1987), 3.
8. Bennett, 32.
9. James B. Simpson, *Simpson's Contemporary Quotations* (Boston: Houghton-Mifflin, 1988), 120.
10. John Rae, *Letters from School* (London: Collins, 1987), Preface, 15.
11. Howard Means, "The Mystery of a Good School," *The Washingtonian,* November 1981, 96.
12. Patrick Welsh, *Tales Out of School* (New York: Penguin Books, 1986), 114–15.
13. Richard J. Light, *The Harvard Assessment Seminars* (Cambridge: Harvard University, 1990), 8–10.

14. Robert Bolt, *A Man for All Seasons* (New York: Vintage Books, 1962), 6.

Chapter Six

1. *Time,* May 25, 1987.
2. For a thoughtful discussion of Locke's contribution to American thought, see Robert N. Bellah, Richard Madsen, William M. Sullivan, Ann Swidler, and Steven M. Tipton, *Habits of the Heart* (New York: Harper and Row, 1985).
3. Bellah et al., 47.
4. Allan Bloom, *The Closing of the American Mind* (New York: Simon and Schuster, 1987).
5. John Silber, *Straight Shooting* (New York: Harper and Row, 1989), 4, 6, 7, 10, 11.

Chapter Seven

1. Edwin Fishel, Letters to the Editor, *The Washington Post,* September 22, 1988, A24.
2. Richard Hawley, *About Boys' Schools* (Hunting Valley, Ohio: University School, 1990), 3.
3. A. Bryk and V. Lee, "Effects of Single Sex Secondary Schools on Student Achievement and Attitudes," *Journal of Educational Psychology,* vol. 78, no. 5.
4. Oral report made at 2nd Annual Boys' Schools Conversation, April 1990.
5. Hawley, 25–26.
6. Patrick Welsh, *Tales Out of School* (New York: Penguin Books, 1986), 205.

Chapter Eight

1. Diane Ravitch, "Well, Maybe We Deserve It," *The Washington Post,* October 25, 1988, A27.
2. Exodus 20:1–2.
3. "David Aloian," *Concord Academy Magazine* (Concord, Mass.: Spring 1987), 4–5.

Index

About the Author

Mark H. Mullin has been Headmaster of St. Albans School in Washington, D.C. since 1977. He was educated at Harvard, Oxford, and General Theological Seminary in New York, and is an ordained Priest in the Episcopal Church. He is a dynamic, respected leader in secondary education, and has more than twenty years' experience as teacher and headmaster of prominent schools.

St. Albans, which opened in 1909 and is the Choir School for the Washington Cathedral, is one of the leading day schools in the United States.